MAY   2007

D1509306

jeff nathan's family suppers

jeff nathan's family suppers

More Than 125 Simple Kosher Recipes

Jeff Nathan

Photographs by Alan Richardson

CLARKSON POTTER/PUBLISHERS
NEW YORK

Copyright © 2005 by Jeffrey Nathan
Photographs copyright © 2005 by Alan Richardson

Published in the United States by Clarkson Potter/Publishers, an imprint
of the Crown Publishing Group, a division of Random House, Inc., New York.
www.crownpublishing.com
www.clarksonpotter.com

CLARKSON N. POTTER is a trademark and POTTER and colophon
are registered trademarks of Random House, Inc.

Library of Congress Cataloging-in-Publication Data
Nathan, Jeff.
Jeff Nathan's family suppers : more than 125 simple kosher recipes / Jeff Nathan.
Includes index.
1. Cookery, Jewish.   I. Title: Family suppers.   II. Title.
TX724
[b.N3663   2005]
641.5'676—dc22   2004029794

ISBN 1-4000-8161-0

Printed in the United States of America

Design by Jane Treuhaft

2   4   6   8   10   9   7   5   3   1

First Edition

This book is dedicated to those I love . . .
My wife, Alison, who has constantly been by my side in all that I do,
giving me support, confidence, and love.

And our kids, Chad and Jaclyn, simply because I love them!

They are unconditional in their love, unwavering in their support,
and unreserved in their belief in me.

They are my passion and my inspiration.

ACKNOWLEDGMENTS

One of the best parts about writing this cookbook is that I was able to eat many meals with my family. Meals that, as a restaurateur, I would normally have missed. No matter how many oohs and aahs I get from my customers, no response is more satisfying than the one I get from my wife, Alison, and our kids, Chad and Jaclyn. They encourage me and fill me with the love and confidence to do all that I dream of. For that, I will always be grateful.

Special thanks are due to my great partners, Harvey and Bob. Harvey Riezenman and I have been partners for two and a half decades and through half a dozen restaurants. He and his wife, Charlotte, are our extended family. Bob and Frances Ross, the balance of our group, have continually offered encouragement and support.

Though the restaurant business varies with the seasons, my fortune in having the loyalty and trustworthiness of my staff has been constant. In a restaurant and catering establishment as large as Abigael's, there are a lot of people working for me who, in turn, allowed me to work on this and many other projects. My general manager, Jigi Mathew, has always been passionate and dedicated. Thank you, Jigi, for your tireless work and loyalty to me and the Abigael's Group. I must thank my chef de cuisine, Ramon Mercedes; my banquet chef, Jose (Tony) Guzman; and my café manager, David Frank, all of whom are invaluable! Their enthusiasm and talents have helped me to achieve my goals and continue to expand our opportunities in so many other areas. My cooks, Junior Nicasio, Eric Pablo, Domingo Guiterrez, and Chico Martinez, all work way beyond the call of duty to help us become more successful. A kosher restaurant wouldn't be kosher without its Mashgiach (kosher supervisor); Mendy Segal and Reuben Barzanfarg share this important role. My manager, Ozzie Cabrera, keeps the front of the house running as smooth as it could possibly be. Thanks also to Mary Goldstein, who, with her willingness to always help, is a treasure. And to the many waiters, waitresses, busboys, prep cooks, dishwashers, and student interns who kept Abigael's running at a top-notch level whether I was present or not; to all of you, I give my utmost thanks for your diligent work and devotion.

On the off chance that we didn't have enough to do, the very same year that I spent writing this cookbook, we began expanding into the catering business. No easy task, even without all the other ventures I'm involved in! Therefore, I must include in my list of thank-yous a few more wonderful people. My event planners, Alisha Adi Katz and Barbara Horvath, are invaluable. Our partners, Stuart and Caryn Morginstin, have helped to make our first year run well.

Special thanks are due to my good friend Rick Rodgers. He shines in the culinary world as a cookbook author and teacher. Rick translated my unwavering passion for food into the written word. He is a master at his craft and I am honored to work with him.

Bob Tabian, my literary agent, deserves many thanks for taking care of all the ins, outs, ups, and downs of writing a cookbook. I am grateful for all the help he provided.

Pam Krauss has once again been a pleasure to work with. Rica Allannic and Jennifer DeFilippi, our newfound friends and editors, have been invaluable in the production of this book. The Clarkson Potter team deserves a big thank-you for all the attention to detail shown in every aspect of this cookbook.

I am grateful for the generosity of the Dacor Company, and especially to Ken Tangredi, district manager. Right in the midst of testing these 125 or so recipes, my well-worn oven baked its last bun! Within days, Dacor had me equipped with the most fabulous equipment they carry. The backyard grill

is the most amazing unit I have ever worked with. Barbecues will never be the same again at our house! I am forever grateful for their generosity and assistance in making the recipe testing of this book such a pleasure. (Recipe testing for book three is about to begin!)

The photographs by Alan Richardson are as fantastic as I knew they would be. His creative style and amazing talent really heighten the look of this book. Envisioning and creating these images at the studio and in my home with Alan was a great experience!

I would also like to thank my food stylist, Anne Disrude, for her expertise and attention to detail. The photos look good enough to eat!

There are many others that may not have cooked with me, washed dishes, or helped out with the grocery shopping, but I am indebted to them nonetheless for their support and encouragement for every new venture I make. For that unwavering support I must thank my in-laws Monney and Selina Siegel. Their confidence in us is unparalleled, except perhaps by their confidence in all their other kids! Thanks also for all the support from my many sisters- and brothers-in-law.

For their abounding love and belief in me, my appreciation to my parents, Harriet Nathan and Herb and Elena Nathan. And to sister Shelly (and Sal, too!), I offer my love and my thanks.

Through my work as chef/host of the television series *New Jewish Cuisine,* I have achieved many things that chefs only dream of. In the process, I made some great friends. Harvey Lehrer and Jay Sanderson, I thank you both for your continued support and encouragement in all that I do.

New Jewish Cuisine connected me with the Hain Celestial Corporation. Ellen Deutsch, in seeking me out, opened up new opportunities for me—

opportunities that I hadn't even yet had a chance to dream of. Ellen, you will forever be my angel. Irwin Simon, CEO of the Hain Celestial Corporation, you have become an employer, a mentor, and a friend. I am honored to be a part of your team.

Many thanks are offered to Rabbis Harvey, Danny, and Ari Senter, at the Kof-K Supervisory Board. Rabbi Yossi Abercasis, the head supervisor for Abigael's, is always great to work with. In the process, he's become a good friend, too. He has tirelessly answered my questions about kashrus and Judaism, while feeding me a much enjoyed diet of food for thought, food for spirit, and food for the soul. It's a good thing I like to learn as well as eat!

No thanks are complete without thanking the higher powers that have bestowed upon me good grace and good fortune. I have been blessed with the ones I love. I have been blessed in my career. I am forever grateful.

CONTENTS

INTRODUCTION

Every night, millions of families struggle to put a flavorful, healthful dinner on the table. I know, because even though my family loves to cook together, finding time to create the evening meal can be a challenge. And night after night, we confront the same question that countless other families do: What's for dinner?

Compounding the issue is the upgrading of the American palate. With television cooking shows (including my *New Jewish Cuisine* series) exposing every family member to great food, people just do not want to settle for boring meals. This ups the ante for the family's main cook—who may or may not be Mom. Nothing kills a family's appetite more than predictability, where Monday is *always* Meat Loaf Night. Variety may be the spice of life, but never more so than when you are living a good portion of that life eating.

To add more to the pot, consider the results of studies that show how the simple act of sharing a meal at the end of the day bonds family members like no other experience. Or other studies that report on the growing problem of child obesity, relative to the number of visits kids (and their parents) make to fast-food franchises where fatty burgers and fries substitute for a well-balanced homemade meal.

In other words, family suppers are too important to ignore.

In *Jeff Nathan's Family Suppers: More Than 125 Simple Kosher Recipes*, the recipes naturally reflect my sensibilities as a trained chef. But I have also worked very hard to keep this book as practical as possible for the busy home cook. While I never compromise on flavor by limiting the number of ingredients or cutting corners on quality, I keep a close watch on such important elements as availability, preparation effort, and cooking time. For example, we bought the groceries for recipe testing at our neighborhood market, resisting the temptation to bring home restaurant ingredients, because what is available wholesale is usually much different than what the home cook can find.

While many recipes are quick sautés, stir-fries, and grilled dishes, not every one is fast-cooking, simply because some foods (such as the meat cuts required by kosher dietary law and many home-style favorites) need long simmering for tenderizing and to bring out flavor. With these slow-cooked dishes, remember that the cook is usually rewarded with enough food for more than one meal.

Each recipe is marked dairy, meat, or pareve. When a recipe can be easily changed from one category to another with a few simple substitutions, I give the directions for making the switch. You'll find satisfying soups and salads that are complete meals; fabulous dishes with poultry, meat, and fish; vegetarian recipes for meatless suppers; pastas and side dishes. And because any day that has a homemade dessert in it automatically seems a bit brighter, the book wraps up with a wide range of desserts, from cookies to blintzes. (Yes, blintzes, for dessert.)

Along the way, I share tips for getting your family around the table for a meal. You'll find ways to organize time, so meals require less preparation, and tips on projects that can get the whole family involved in the cooking

process. I've also provided information that highlights my "most useful" ingredients, such as mushrooms and fresh herbs.

These are the recipes that my wife, Ali, and I make every night, along with our two kids, Chad and Jackie. I feel sorry for kids whose idea of cooking is heating up a meal in the microwave. That's not cooking, that's reheating! My kids help us wash produce, chop onions, measure out dry goods, set the table, wash the dishes . . . and they love it. (In fact, Chad is hinting that he might want to go to chef's school. Now I know how actors feel when their child says he wants to be in the movies.)

When kids cook, they learn so many skills that it's hard to count them all: math (Ali: "There are 16 tablespoons to a cup, so if you want ¾ cup, how much is that?"); hygiene (Dad: "Hey, wash those hands before you handle the food!"); etiquette (Jackie sets a mean table with the silverware lined up perfectly according to Miss Manners' guidelines); developing personal taste (Jackie: "Dad, maybe a bit less curry the next time . . ."), and creativity (Chad: "I think I'll make up my own recipe for curried chicken. Okay?"). Of course, nutritional choices play a big role in what we make for supper. Variety is important, not only to expose kids to the many different foods they'll encounter as grown-ups, but also to help them make smart, healthful choices about eating on their own.

Commerce was an unexpected skill that the kids learned in our kitchen. I like to make sandwiches for Chad and Jackie's lunch boxes, and I would have fun surprising them with new offerings. We found out that their sandwiches were so popular that the kids started selling them to their classmates! So that Dad wouldn't have another commissary to run on his hands, we put an end to the practice.

I work many evenings, so the supper time I have with my family is precious. Cooking together gives us quality time of the highest order. Coming home to a great group of people is wonderful. Coming home to sit around the table sharing a delicious, carefully prepared meal with people you love is heaven on earth. So, here they are: the Nathan family's favorites. I hope they will have your family asking for seconds, too!

Jeff Nathan
www.abigaels.com
September 2005

Our kitchen was built for a family that loves to cook together. In other words, function takes precedence over design—it isn't fancy, but it works. However, when I peek into the cabinets and look at the appliances, I see places where our chef-trained sensibilities definitely informed certain purchasing decisions. It used to be that only chefs were concerned about triple-ply cookware and the amount of BTUs in a stove burner, but not anymore. Sure, you can make good food with middle-of-the-road cookware and appliances, but upgrades in certain areas will make your time in the kitchen more efficient and more fun.

If there is one time when I recommend that you buy the best, it is when you are purchasing the stove. Recently, we bought a Dacor range with a convection oven (which cuts roasting and baking times by about a third) and high-heat burners (which also speed up cooking as well as provide skillet-cooked food with a deliciously browned crust). Now that we have a great Dacor stove, we wonder how we did without one for so long. If you want a microwave oven, consider a microwave/convection combination so you can really pull it into action to cook your favorite dishes; the typical microwave without convection requires the cook to make many alterations to conventional recipes, and the results are iffy at best.

Having the right pots and pans can make an enormous difference in your cooking. I occasionally teach cooking classes in private homes. After struggling to cook meals for twelve guests in the hostess's tiny frying pans, I started bringing my own utensils. Heavy-gauge metal cookware cooks most evenly, and it is well worth the investment.

Be sure to buy the correct-size cookware to fit the needs of your family. Every kitchen should have a large, 12-inch heavy-gauge skillet. One of these babies will hold an entire cut-up chicken or four lamb chops without crowding. You should also have a 6- to 8-quart Dutch oven for braising stews; a 2- to 3-quart saucepan for side dishes; and a 1- to 2-quart saucepan to cook smaller amounts of food. You will find more uses for a very large (8- to 12-quart) soup kettle than you might expect, from making big batches of soup to boiling lots of water for a double batch of pasta. These are just the basics, and the list should be amended according to your budget, cooking habits, and storage space. But get that big skillet, or two if you can!

We also rely on a standing heavy-duty electric mixer and a food processor, but those are hardly gourmet appliances these days. For everyday cooking, the mixer is a big help because you don't have to stand over it while it's working, freeing you to do another task. (We do use a hand mixer for small jobs, such as whipping a little heavy cream or a few egg whites.) On lazy days, we love to bake bread, and the large mixer makes easy work of kneading the dough. My food processor is used almost every day to prep vegetables, shred cheese, and more—it takes about one-fourth of the time to ready the vegetables for latkes and coleslaw with a food processor than it does by hand, and no grated knuckles, either!

There are three other appliances that I have to recommend. I love my immersion blender (the handheld ones that look like a thick wand) for puréeing food right in the cooking pot. And an inexpensive electric juicer will amaze you with how fast it can juice fruit, straining out the seeds, too. And because I like to create my own seasoning blends (and because whole spices have so much more flavor than the previously ground kind), a spice grinder is very useful.

The four of us like to cook together, so we have a lot of cutting boards. Dividing up the different cooking jobs, with one of us chopping onions while another does the herbs, also cuts way down on the prep time. Plastic boards are easy to keep clean and most are dishwasher-safe. On the other hand, wooden boards are very sturdy, and studies have shown that neither one is more sanitary than the other. So the choice is yours.

Be picky about your knives. It's true that you can get by with three knives in your kitchen. A chef's knife is for major cutting, slicing, and chopping. Recently, I have found a similar knife that I prefer to the classic French chef's knife. It's slightly serrated, with a rounded nose and holds its edge like no other knife I've ever used, making it perfect for a huge range of jobs. In fact, I liked it so much that I offer it in my cutlery line at www.abigaels.com. You should also have a smaller utility knife, which is great for trimming skin from poultry and fish, and dealing with small items or delicate produce. A paring knife . . . well, it pares thick skin from veggies and fruits. A serrated knife for slicing bread and thin-skinned tomatoes should be added to the list.

Look for a knife that is forged from a solid piece of metal, and not one where the blade is stuck into a handle. When buying a knife, it's important to hold it in your hand to evaluate its weight and balance relative to your own build and style—sometimes a smaller or larger knife would be better. And once you have your knife, keep it sharp! Remember that you are supposed to keep the blade consistently sharp. Buy a sharpening steel and use it often, not just when the blade gets dull.

So, don't make your cooking a struggle by using substandard utensils and kitchenware. A lot of cooks sentimentally cling to every culinary hand-me-down that has come down through the ages and into their kitchens. Buying the best you can afford when setting up your kitchen will save you time and money in the long run. Upgrade by treating yourself to special pots and pans whenever you can—a wedding anniversary, a Hanukkah present, and especially something new and shiny for every Passover.

Perhaps the biggest asset in preparing daily family meals is a well-stocked pantry. Don't fill up the shopping cart during every trip to the market. When shopping in bulk, stock up on pantry items, such as canned beans, pasta, and the like, whenever you do have extra space in the cart. When stopping to pick up groceries after work, the goal should be to get only a few fresh items (meat and vegetables) so you can get out of there and into your kitchen as quickly as possible.

Cooking for a kosher home has its own considerations. Because I have often run out of seasonal groceries like matzo meal, potato starch, and matzo farfel in the middle of a recipe, I now get an extra box or two whenever I see them at my local supermarket (depending where you live, sometimes they're only available during the Passover season). But the big news is the increasing range of ethnic ingredients that are becoming available to the kosher home cook—I am amazed at the labels that now sport a hechsher, the symbol of kosher supervision. These products offer more possibilities than ever for cooking with flavors from all over the world. Remember, to keep your family interested in what's on the dinner table, you need to vary the menu, and not just serve the same-old, same-old. So get creative with your cooking and take advantage of these global groceries.

Here are some of the things that I can't cook without. The list could go on, but these are the items that are used most in this book. I have left out the obvious flour, eggs, sugar and the like. The "Could-Haves" are optional ingredients that I want to encourage you to have on hand. They may be a bit esoteric, but they will add an incredible amount of flavor to your cooking. Once they are in your pantry, you will come to enjoy experimenting with new tastes and textures—and your family will thank you for it.

Flavorings

Kosher salt This coarse-grained salt has a clean, unadulterated flavor and is easy to pick up with your fingers for sprinkling over food.

Sea salt Offers an oceanic flavor to complement fish.

Whole black peppercorns Left whole for stocks and ground in a peppermill for seasoning.

Dark sesame oil Don't confuse this with the clear gold variety, which has less flavor.

Red wine vinegar The best brands have a more rounded wine flavor and less bite.

Balsamic vinegar Indispensable for its slightly sweet note.

Cider vinegar A bit sharper than its cousins; a splash on baked bean dishes can really perk them up.

Dijon mustard Provides a lively mustard flavor.

Spicy brown "deli-style" mustard For when old-fashioned flavor is important.

Soy sauce You can't cook Asian cuisine without it; if you prefer, you can use low-sodium.

COULD-HAVES

Canned anchovies in oil A couple of chopped anchovies provide a well-rounded but elusive saltiness.

Capers in brine Their bitterness complements other strong flavors, such as anchovies, garlic, and olives.

Dried porcini With an earthy flavor that can't be duplicated, these mushrooms are usually soaked and drained before using.

Wasabi powder A type of green horse-radish, it came to this country as a condiment for sushi, but its sinus-clearing heat can also be used to flavor unsuspecting dishes such as mashed potatoes.

Rice wine vinegar This mild vinegar lends a distinctive Asian flavor to many dishes. You'll find it in the Asian section of your market.

Canned and Dry Goods

Extra-virgin olive oil This has the fullest flavor of all the olive oils, and can be used for most cooking and for dressing salads; use a reasonably priced supermarket brand. For everyday sautéing, a plain olive oil is fine.

Chicken broth or bouillon I use chicken broth or reconstituted bouillon as my all-purpose cooking liquid because I haven't found a kosher beef broth convenience product that I like.

Vegetable bouillon or powder There is canned vegetable broth on the market, but I find that the bouillon cubes have the best flavor.

Canned beans I always have chickpeas, black beans, and white kidney beans (cannellini) on hand.

Canned tomatoes I like to have both crushed tomatoes and chopped tomatoes in juice, because of their different textures.

Tomato paste Adds another layer of flavor to tomato-based dishes.

Canned tuna This standby finds its way into salads, sandwiches, and pasta.

Dried bread crumbs Keep both plain and seasoned on hand to do a variety of jobs, from coating food to binding meat loaf and meatballs.

Matzo meal For the times you can't use bread crumbs and want an added texture.

Matzo flour and potato starch Both musts for Passover baking.

High-quality dried pasta Although it's more expensive, I much prefer the flavor and texture of imported Italian pasta.

COULD-HAVES

Panko One of my favorite ingredients, these crisp Japanese bread crumbs create extra-crunchy coatings.

Almond paste A must-have for Passover, keep a couple of extra cans on hand for other dessert recipes (like my Almond Mini Muffins on page 212).

Refrigerated and Frozen Foods

Unsalted butter A must for baking and dairy sautés. There's very little margarine in my kitchen.

Heavy cream Have a half-pint on hand for desserts and dairy meals; after all, it lasts a few weeks.

Frozen nondairy whipped topping For when you want to serve a creamy dessert at the end of a meat meal.

Frozen corn kernels and frozen peas These are great for adding color and flavor to many savory dishes.

Mayonnaise This condiment may be a little bland on its own, so I add other flavors to jazz it up.

Kalamata olives Just a few will bring the Mediterranean to your table; look for pitted olives.

Parmesan cheese You'll get the best flavor from a chunk of cheese, not the pregrated kind.

COULD-HAVES

Homemade compound butters (see page 129) These give so much flavor for so little effort that everyone should have them in their freezer.

Homemade condiments (see page 179) Use them on your sandwiches; stir them into salad dressings or sauces.

Produce

Yellow and red onions These root vegetables create the backbone to many dishes; be sure to get true yellow (sometimes called Spanish) onions, and not Vidalia, which can be too sweet.

Shallots Small but packed with flavor; a must-have for many recipes from dressings to soups.

Seasoning
Koshered Meat and Poultry

The recipes in this book assume that your meat and poultry will come from kosher butchers, where it will have been salted according to kashering practice. This procedure leaves the food seasoned, and it is generally not sprinkled with salt again during cooking. Instead, the meat and poultry dishes are seasoned at the end of cooking, according to your taste, with pepper and additional salt, if needed. When a dish cannot be tasted (say, at the beginning of a recipe when the ingredients are raw), I provide a measured amount of salt, according to my taste, still leaving some leeway for your personalized seasoning at the end of the cooking.

Garlic The more, the better as far as I'm concerned. Don't get elephant garlic, which has no flavor.

Lemons Squeeze them over fish and juice them for salad dressings.

Limes For a tropical citrus flavor, limes can't be beat.

Oranges Navel oranges are the most versatile, because they have a lot of juice, can be easily cut into sections for salads, and have a thick peel with a zest that is easy to remove.

Fresh parsley A sprinkle of chopped fresh parsley can really brighten up the look and flavor of a drab dish.

Fresh basil, thyme, and rosemary I always have at least one of these fragrant beauties in my refrigerator.

Carrots and celery I put these two together because they are often found in the same recipe; they are also healthy before-dinner snacks.

Potatoes Use either all-purpose brown-skinned or red boiling potatoes to add bulk to stews and casseroles.

Mushrooms See note on page 35.

The Spice Cabinet

Keep these in a cool, dark place (not near the stove!) and replace every six months, as they will lose their flavor with age.

Dried basil What is Italian cooking without it?

Dried oregano This has a much zestier flavor than the fresh version.

Dried rosemary Good to have around when fresh isn't in the refrigerator.

Herbes de Provence A blend of basil, thyme, rosemary, and fennel, often with savory and lavender; if you can't find it, substitute equal parts of the first three, plus a pinch of fennel seed.

Chili powder A blend of ground chiles, with cumin, garlic, and other seasonings.

Curry powder One of the most aromatic of all spice blends.

Ground cinnamon Not just for desserts, it adds spicy warmth to savory dishes.

Ground cumin This spice is familiar in Mexican cooking, but found in Indian and Middle Eastern recipes, too.

Fennel seed My secret ingredient, I sneak a bit into dishes for a hint of anise flavor; especially good with fish.

Hot red pepper flakes I use these when I want the hot flavor in a dish to have more Mediterranean personality than black pepper would deliver.

Cayenne pepper For when I need the spiciness to really make a statement!

COULD-HAVES

Saffron Expensive (it's very difficult to harvest), but worth having for its unique flavor; buy it in small quantities.

Pure ground chile powder Unlike chili powder, which has other ingredients, these are unadulterated ground chiles. I use sweet/hot ancho and over-the-top/hot chipotle most often in my cooking.

soups

In these days of instant cooking, soup stubbornly refuses to change according to fashion. A long, slow simmer is the only way for it to develop the old-fashioned flavor that we all crave. A leisurely weekend afternoon is the perfect time to cook up a pot, where it can bubble quietly without anyone keeping an anxious eye on the clock. Not only will your masterpiece provide a couple of meals, you can also hope to have leftovers to freeze for another time. Making a pot of soup is even more appropriate as a rainy-weekend project because chopping up the required amount of vegetables can keep the kids busy (not that adults don't get cabin fever, too).

Soup can play many roles in a family's menu plan. How many cases of the sniffles have been chased away by a steaming bowl of homemade soup? Served hot, soup sustains and comforts during cold weather, and served chilled when it's muggy outside, it can restore and refresh. It has long been a mainstay for lunch, but it shouldn't be overlooked as a light supper. As the kettle simmers on top of the stove, fogging up the kitchen windows, keep the cooking going by baking biscuits to serve with your meal. Expose your family to homemade soup with biscuits fresh from the oven, and they may be spoiled for life against processed foods—which wouldn't be such a bad thing.

beef, barley, and potato soup

MAKES 8 TO 10 SERVINGS

Whenever I make this soup, it reminds me of the best kind of "Grandma" food—comforting, filling, and delicious. Parboiling the barley and beef gives the barley a firmer, less slick texture, and removes excess fat from the beef.

1 pound ground beef

¾ cup pearled barley

3 tablespoons olive oil

2 medium onions, chopped

3 medium carrots, chopped

3 garlic cloves, minced

1½ teaspoons caraway seeds

2 quarts chicken broth

4 medium baking potatoes, such as Burbank or russet, peeled and cut into ½-inch pieces

¼ cup chopped fresh parsley

Kosher salt and freshly ground black pepper to taste

PAREVE VARIATION

Omit the ground beef and make the soup with Vegetable Broth (page 44) or vegetable bouillon.

1. Bring a large saucepan of water to a boil over high heat. Add the ground beef and cook, stirring constantly to break the meat into small pieces, until the meat loses its raw look, about 5 minutes. Drain in a large colander.

2. Bring a medium saucepan of water to a boil over high heat. Stir in the barley and cook for 5 minutes; the barley does not have to soften. Drain in a wire sieve, rinse under cold water, and drain again.

3. Heat the oil in a large pot over medium heat. Add the onions and cook, stirring occasionally, until they are translucent, about 5 minutes. Add the carrots, garlic, and caraway seeds. Reduce the heat to medium-low and cook, stirring often, until the carrots begin to soften, about 5 minutes. Stir in the broth, potatoes, and reserved barley. Bring to a boil over high heat.

4. Reduce the heat to medium-low. Simmer for 25 minutes. Add the reserved beef and cook until the potatoes are very tender, about 15 minutes more. Stir in the parsley. Season with salt and pepper. Serve hot.

tuscan vegetable soup

MAKES 8 TO 10 SERVINGS

This light and fragrant soup is similar to that superstar of Italian cookery, minestrone. However, my version skips the pork (many recipes include prosciutto), an omission that is not missed at all when such a profusion of vegetables comes into play. I purposely mix dried oregano with the fresh basil. The former has a familiar sharpness that the fresh version just doesn't deliver.

⅓ cup plus 1 tablespoon olive oil

2 medium onions, chopped

6 medium carrots, chopped

3 medium celery ribs, chopped

¼ head green cabbage, cored and coarsely chopped (about 3 cups)

½ head escarole, trimmed and coarsely chopped (about 4 cups)

1 cup tomato paste

1 tablespoon dried oregano

6 garlic cloves, finely chopped

3 quarts Vegetable Broth (page 44), vegetable bouillon, or water

Two 15- to 19-ounce cans cannellini (white kidney) beans, drained and rinsed

1 medium zucchini, chopped

⅓ cup chopped fresh basil

Kosher salt and freshly ground black pepper to taste

1. Heat the oil in a soup pot over medium heat. Add the onions, carrots, celery, cabbage, and escarole. Cook, stirring often, until the vegetables soften, about 15 minutes.

2. Stir in the tomato paste, oregano, and garlic. Cook, stirring often, until the vegetables are tender (but take care not to scorch the tomato paste), about 7 minutes more. Stir in the broth and bring to a boil over high heat. Stir in the beans and zucchini.

3. Reduce the heat to medium-low and simmer until the zucchini is tender and the soup liquid is slightly thickened, about 20 minutes. Stir in the basil or mixed herbs. Season with salt and pepper. Serve hot.

cuban black bean soup

MAKES 12 SERVINGS

Making this dramatically dark, spicy bean soup in meat, pareve, or dairy versions is always tasty. (The pastrami meat seasoning may not be Cuban, but it sure is good.) Be sure to use dried black beans, because they have a color, flavor, and texture that the canned can't deliver.

1 pound dried black beans, sorted over for stones, rinsed, and drained

$\frac{1}{3}$ cup plus 2 tablespoons extra-virgin olive oil

2 medium onions, chopped

4 medium carrots, chopped

2 medium celery ribs, chopped

$\frac{1}{2}$ pound sliced pastrami ($\frac{1}{4}$-inch thick), cut into $\frac{1}{4}$-inch dice

1 tablespoon ground cumin

8 garlic cloves, minced

1 jalapeño, seeded and minced

1 gallon water

Kosher salt and freshly ground black pepper to taste

$\frac{1}{2}$ cup chopped fresh cilantro

1. At least 8 hours before cooking, place the beans in a large bowl and add enough cold water to cover the beans by 2 inches. Let stand at room temperature (if the kitchen is warm, refrigerate the bowl of beans) for 8 to 12 hours. (For a quicker alternative, see Note.) Drain well.

2. Heat the oil in a large pot over medium heat. Add the onions, carrots, and celery and cook, stirring often, until the vegetables are softened, about 12 minutes. Stir in the pastrami, cumin, garlic, and jalapeño. Reduce the heat to low and cook until the jalapeño softens, 5 to 7 minutes. Add the drained beans. Stir in the water. Bring to a boil over high heat.

3. Reduce the heat to medium-low. Simmer until the beans are very tender, about $1\frac{1}{4}$ hours. During the last 15 minutes, season with salt and pepper.

4. In batches, transfer the soup to a blender and purée. (Or use a handheld immersion blender to process the soup right in the pot.) Transfer the batches of puréed soup to a serving bowl. Stir in the cilantro and season again with salt and pepper. Serve hot.

NOTE For the best results, soak the beans overnight. But if you forget or you're in a hurry, the beans can be boiled in water to cover for 2 minutes, removed from the heat, covered, and allowed to stand for 1 hour. Drain, and you're good to go!

PAREVE VARIATION

Omit the pastrami. Season the soup with 1 teaspoon kosher salt when adding the water, then adjust the seasonings after puréeing the soup. Garnish with thinly sliced scallions.

DAIRY VARIATION

Omit the pastrami. Season the soup with 1 teaspoon kosher salt when adding the water, then adjust the seasonings after puréeing the soup. Garnish the soup with dollops of sour cream and sliced scallions.

mediterranean fish soup

MAKES 8 SERVINGS

This aromatic soup gets its depth of flavor from fish stock, which is so much quicker to make than chicken or meat stock. Make the stock the day before, and you'll have the soup on the table in less than an hour. If you'd like to make this a bit more substantial for a main-course soup, add a third of a cup of pasta, such as ditalini, to the soup during the last 15 minutes of cooking.

⅓ cup plus 1 tablespoon extra-virgin olive oil

4 garlic cloves, chopped

½ teaspoon hot red pepper flakes

1 large onion, chopped

4 medium carrots, chopped

2 large leeks, white and pale green parts only, chopped and well rinsed

½ small fennel bulb, cored and chopped (about 1 cup)

One 28-ounce can crushed tomatoes

2 quarts Fish Stock (page 43)

4 medium red-skinned potatoes, cut into ¾-inch dice

2 pounds firm, white-fleshed, skinless fish fillets, such as halibut and cod, cut into ¾-inch chunks

¼ cup chopped fresh parsley

1 teaspoon chopped fresh thyme or ½ teaspoon dried thyme

1 teaspoon chopped fresh tarragon or ½ teaspoon dried tarragon

Kosher salt and freshly ground black pepper to taste

1. Heat the oil in a soup kettle over medium-low heat. Add the garlic and red pepper flakes and cook just until the garlic is beginning to color, about 2 minutes. Add the onion, carrots, leeks, and fennel. Cook, uncovered, stirring often, until the vegetables are translucent, about 10 minutes. Stir in the tomatoes, and bring to a boil over medium-high heat.

2. Add the fish stock and potatoes, and bring to a simmer over high heat. Return the heat to medium-low and simmer until the potatoes are tender, about 30 minutes.

3. Stir the fish, parsley, thyme, and tarragon into the soup and cook just until the fish turns opaque, about 5 minutes. Season the soup with salt and pepper. Serve immediately.

NOTE Before cutting the fish fillets into chunks, run your fingertips over both sides to feel for any thin bones that the fishmonger may have missed. If you find some, pull them out with thin-nosed pliers (wash the pliers well and hold over an open flame for a few seconds to sterilize). Many kitchenware shops now carry tweezers that are specially made for removing fish bones. If you cook a lot of fish, they are a good investment.

garbanzo bean and cilantro soup

MAKES 8 SERVINGS

This is known as "falafel soup" in our house, because the flavors remind us of that famous Israeli snack. Canned garbanzo beans are an indispensable pantry item, for adding to everything from soups to salads—and, of course, for making falafel. Home-made vegetable broth or reconstituted vegetable bouillon will give the best results, but I have also made this with water alone.

2 tablespoons extra-virgin olive oil

1 medium onion, finely chopped

Two 15- to 19-ounce cans garbanzo beans (chickpeas), drained and rinsed

1 large baking potato, such as Burbank or russet, peeled and cut into ½-inch dice

1 medium carrot, finely chopped

3 garlic cloves, chopped

1 tablespoon curry powder

½ teaspoon ground cumin

1½ quarts Vegetable Broth (page 44), vegetable bouillon, or water

3 tablespoons chopped fresh cilantro

Kosher salt and freshly ground black pepper to taste

1. Heat the oil in a large pot over medium heat. Add the onion and cook, stirring occasionally, until it is golden, about 7 minutes. Add the beans, potato, carrot, garlic, curry powder, and cumin and reduce the heat to medium-low. Cook, stirring often, until the carrots soften, about 5 minutes.

2. Stir in the vegetable broth, scraping up the film on the bottom of the pot. Bring to a boil over high heat. Reduce the heat to medium-low. Simmer until the potato is very tender, about 25 minutes.

3. In batches, transfer the soup to a blender and pulse just until the soup is chunky—do not purée. (Or use a handheld immersion blender to process the soup right in the pot.) Transfer the batches of puréed soup to a serving bowl. Stir in the cilantro and season with salt and pepper. Serve hot.

chilled sweet pepper and pineapple soup

MAKES 6 TO 8 SERVINGS

We like to serve this family favorite at backyard barbecues, where the combination of sweet pineapple, spicy peppers, and sharp cilantro is always a conversation-maker to the uninitiated. Make it early in the morning so it will be well chilled by supper time. In a rush, I'll put the soup in a large bowl and bury it in a larger bowl of ice, where it will chill very quickly.

$\frac{1}{2}$ **large pineapple, pared, cored, and cut into $\frac{1}{4}$-inch dice (6 cups)**

2 small red bell peppers, cored, seeded, and cut into $\frac{1}{4}$-inch dice (2 cups)

2 small yellow bell peppers, cored, seeded, and cut into $\frac{1}{4}$-inch dice (2 cups)

$\frac{1}{2}$ **seedless English cucumber, cut into $\frac{1}{4}$-inch dice (2 cups)**

$2\frac{2}{3}$ **cups canned pineapple juice (about half of a 46-ounce can)**

$1\frac{1}{2}$ **tablespoons chopped fresh cilantro**

1 jalapeño, seeded and finely chopped

$1\frac{1}{2}$ **teaspoons honey**

Kosher salt to taste

1. Combine 3 cups of pineapple and 1 cup *each* of the red bell pepper, yellow bell pepper, and cucumber in a large stainless-steel or glass bowl. Add $1\frac{1}{3}$ cups pineapple juice. Set aside.

2. Combine the remaining 3 cups pineapple and 1 cup each red bell pepper, yellow bell pepper, and cucumber in a food processor. Process into a purée. Add the remaining $1\frac{1}{3}$ cups pineapple juice, cilantro, jalapeño, and honey, and pulse until smooth. Pour into the bowl of chopped ingredients and mix well. Season very lightly with the salt.

3. Cover and refrigerate for at least 4 hours and up to overnight. Serve chilled.

chicken and tortilla soup

MAKES 8 SERVINGS

Every country has its favorite chicken soup, and this one seems to be the Mexican winner—chunky soup with a crunchy crumbled tortilla topping. I never met a kid who didn't like tortilla chips, so this is a good way to get them to eat nutritious soup. Rather than starting from scratch with a whole chicken, make it with prepared chicken broth and boneless chicken breasts for a quick supper.

$\frac{1}{4}$ cup canola oil

1 large onion, chopped

1 pound boneless, skinless chicken breast, cut into $\frac{1}{2}$-inch pieces

2 medium celery ribs, chopped

1 jalapeño, seeded and minced

1 tablespoon chili powder

$1\frac{1}{2}$ teaspoons Spanish or Hungarian sweet paprika

$1\frac{1}{2}$ teaspoons dried oregano

6 garlic cloves, minced

6 cups chicken broth

One 28-ounce can crushed tomatoes

$2\frac{1}{2}$ cups thawed frozen corn kernels

$\frac{1}{4}$ cup chopped fresh cilantro

Kosher salt to taste

Tortilla chips, for serving

Tomato-Cilantro Salsa (page 162) or store-bought salsa, for serving

1. Heat the oil in a large pot over medium heat. Add the onion and cook, stirring occasionally, until it is translucent, about 5 minutes. Add the chicken, celery, and jalapeño and cook, stirring occasionally, until the celery softens and the chicken is opaque, about 8 minutes. Add the chili powder, paprika, oregano, and garlic. Reduce the heat to low and cook, stirring, until the garlic softens, about 1 minute.

2. Stir in the broth, tomatoes, and corn, scraping up the spices on the bottom of the pot. Bring to a boil over high heat. Reduce the heat to low and simmer until the chicken is cooked through, about 5 minutes. Stir in the cilantro. Season with salt.

3. Ladle the soup into bowls and top each serving with a handful or two of crumbled tortilla chips and a spoonful of salsa. Serve hot with additional salsa passed on the side.

sherried cream of mushroom soup

MAKES 8 SERVINGS

The nutty flavor of dry sherry enhances the earthiness of the mushrooms—leave it out, and the soup will not be the same. If you wish, garnish each serving with some chopped tomato and basil.

1 cup (1 ounce) dried porcini mushrooms

1 cup boiling water

¼ cup extra-virgin olive oil

4 tablespoons (½ stick) unsalted butter

1 small onion, chopped

2 garlic cloves, chopped

2½ pounds assorted fresh mushrooms (such as cremini, pleurottes, stemmed shiitakes, and chanterelles), sliced

⅓ cup all-purpose flour

¼ cup dry sherry

1 tablespoon soy sauce

1 teaspoon sugar

6 cups Vegetable Broth (page 44) or vegetable bouillon

1 cup heavy cream

1 tablespoon dried basil

Kosher salt and freshly ground black pepper to taste

1. Soak the porcini in the boiling water in a small bowl until the mushrooms soften, about 30 minutes. Lift the porcini out of the water and chop coarsely. Strain the soaking liquid through a wire strainer lined with moistened, squeezed-out cheesecloth or a moistened paper towel. Set the mushrooms and liquid aside.

2. Heat the oil and butter in a large pot over medium heat. Add the onion and garlic and cook, stirring occasionally, until the onions soften, about 5 minutes. Add the fresh mushrooms and cook, stirring often, until they release their liquid, about 5 minutes. Sprinkle the flour over the mushrooms and stir well. Stir in the reserved porcini mushrooms and their soaking liquid, sherry, soy sauce, and sugar. Stir in the broth. Bring to a boil over high heat, stirring occasionally. Reduce the heat to medium and simmer for 10 minutes.

3. Stir in the cream and basil. Simmer until the mushrooms are very tender and the soup is well flavored, about 15 minutes more. Season with salt and pepper. Serve hot.

Mushrooms

It wasn't very long ago that when a recipe called for mushrooms, it meant the white button mushroom. Outside of dried mushrooms, which were very difficult to find, it was the only kind of mushroom you could get.

Now my supermarket carries at least five different varieties, and the neighborhood specialty market also supplies wild mushrooms in season. I never know what I'm going to find at the store. But I know one thing: I like to cook with an assortment of mushrooms whenever I can for the depth of flavor, textural variety, and interesting appearance that I don't get when I use just one variety. Here are my favorites:

Brown cremini mushrooms, which are sometimes called baby bellas because they are actually small portobellos, have taken the place of white mushrooms, which I now find too bland, as my all-purpose mushroom.

Large portobello mushrooms have a meaty texture and dark, earthy flavor, and hold up well to grilling.

Shiitakes are full-flavored gems, but be sure to remove their tough stems before using.

Pleurottes, also called oyster mushrooms, have a pale grayish cast, and a delicate flavor.

Tall, thin **enoki mushrooms** are good raw, tucked into salads. Even though the above are referred to as wild mushrooms, these mushrooms are actually cultivated.

True wild mushrooms, such as golden-colored **chanterelles** and elongated **morels,** are available in their respective autumn and spring seasons.

The only dried mushroom I use with any regularity, and they are indispensable in adding extra flavor to soups and stews, is **porcini**—look for whole, unbroken slices.

It's not true that mushrooms can't be washed. In fact, you will certainly want to clean them well, but it should be done quickly and just before using so that the mushrooms don't soak up any water. Place the mushrooms in a colander and rinse under cold running water, moving the mushrooms around under the stream of water, just until the mushrooms look clean. Don't overdo it, or you'll have a soggy batch.

southwestern beef flanken and macaroni soup

MAKES 8 TO 12 SERVINGS

Flanken takes a long time to cook to tenderness, but long-cooked soups are especially flavorful. So, when you have the time to put a pot on the back of the stove to simmer away, consider this spicy soup, laden with chunks of beef and pasta. You won't need broth, as the flanken lends so much taste.

3 tablespoons olive oil, plus more as needed

3 pounds boneless flanken, cut into ¾-inch pieces

3 medium onions, chopped

2 medium carrots, chopped

2 medium celery ribs, chopped

6 garlic cloves, smashed under a knife and peeled

1 tablespoon chili powder

1 teaspoon ground cumin

1 tablespoon dried oregano

2 bay leaves

3 quarts water

Two 28-ounce cans crushed tomatoes

2 large baking potatoes, such as Burbank or russet, scrubbed but unpeeled, cut into ¾-inch pieces

½ pound ditalini pasta

Kosher salt and freshly ground black pepper to taste

1. Heat the oil in a large pot over medium-high heat. In batches, without crowding, add the flanken and cook, turning occasionally, until browned, about 6 minutes. Transfer to a plate.

2. Add more oil to the pot as needed. Add the onions, carrots, celery, and garlic. Reduce the heat to medium and cook, stirring often, until the onions are softened, about 6 minutes. Add the chili powder, cumin, oregano, and bay leaves, and stir for 1 minute, until fragrant. Stir in the water and tomatoes. Return the beef and any juices on the plate to the pot. Bring to a boil over high heat, skimming off any foam that rises to the surface.

3. Reduce the heat to medium-low and simmer until the meat is almost tender, about 1½ hours. Add the potatoes and simmer until both meat and potatoes are tender, about 35 minutes more.

4. Meanwhile, bring a large saucepan of lightly salted water to a boil over high heat. Add the pasta and cook until tender, about 7 minutes. Drain well and add to the soup. Return the soup to a simmer. Season with salt and pepper. Serve hot.

sweet potato and corn chowder

MAKES 8 TO 10 SERVINGS

This extraordinary chowder has a slightly sweet flavor, and gentle spicing provides another element of interest. It's thickened with roasted and puréed sweet potatoes, which bring their own rich taste and color to the proceedings. This would be a great first-course soup for a Thanksgiving feast. Of, if your Thanksgiving meal featured mashed sweet potatoes as a side dish, use about 2½ cups leftover potatoes as a substitute for the roasted ones for a great "day after" soup.

3 large orange-fleshed sweet potatoes (sometimes called yams), such as Louisiana, garnet, or jewel, about 2½ pounds

3 tablespoons canola oil

1 large onion, chopped

2 quarts Vegetable Broth (page 44) or vegetable bouillon

Two 15-ounce cans creamed corn (pareve)

2 tablespoons light brown sugar

¼ teaspoon ground allspice

¼ teaspoon ground cinnamon

¼ cup chopped fresh cilantro

Kosher salt and freshly ground black pepper to taste

1. Position a rack in the center of the oven and preheat to 400°F. Place the sweet potatoes on a rimmed baking sheet. Bake until they are tender, about 1 hour. Protecting your hands with a kitchen towel, peel the potatoes while they are still hot and put the flesh in a medium bowl. Mash them with a potato masher. (Or purée them in a food processor fitted with the metal chopping blade.)

2. Heat the oil in a large pot over medium heat. Add the onion and cook, stirring occasionally, until translucent, about 5 minutes. Stir in the broth, mashed sweet potatoes, creamed corn, brown sugar, allspice, and cinnamon. Bring to a boil over high heat, stirring often to avoid scorching.

3. Reduce the heat to low. Simmer, stirring occasionally, until the soup is well flavored, about 20 minutes. Stir in the cilantro. Season with salt and pepper. Serve hot.

tomato, escarole, and sausage soup

MAKES 6 TO 8 SERVINGS

I am a nut for the slightly bitter flavor of escarole. I use it a lot in soups, and love it as a side dish (see Escarole with Toasted Bread Crumbs on page 198). Fresh escarole has firm, crisp leaves, but it quickly turns tender with simmering. Cooked with tomatoes, Polish sausage, and potatoes, this hearty, vitamin-packed soup is a fine addition to the family supper table.

¼ **cup olive oil**

1 **large yellow onion, coarsely chopped**

12 **garlic cloves, coarsely chopped**

½ **teaspoon hot red pepper flakes**

½ **pound Polish sausage, cut into ½-inch dice**

1 **teaspoon dried basil**

1 **teaspoon dried oregano**

¼ **teaspoon ground fennel seed**

6 **cups chicken broth**

One 28-ounce can crushed tomatoes

1 **head escarole, coarsely chopped into 1- to 2-inch pieces, well rinsed**

1 **large baking potato, such as Burbank or russet, cut into ¾-inch chunks**

Kosher salt and freshly ground black pepper to taste

1. Heat the oil in a large pot over medium heat. Add the onion, garlic, and red pepper flakes. Cook, stirring often, until the onion is translucent, about 5 minutes. Stir in the sausage, basil, oregano, and fennel.

2. Add the broth and tomatoes and bring to a boil over high heat. Stir in the escarole and potato. Reduce the heat to medium-low. Simmer until the potatoes are tender, about 35 minutes (tomatoes inhibit the softening of the potatoes, so they'll take a bit longer than when cooked with broth alone). Season with salt and pepper and serve hot.

Fennel Seed

More common in French kitchens than in American ones, fennel seed is related to anise seed, but with a less sweet, more savory flavor. It gets a workout at the Nathan house; I usually grind it in a spice grinder or mortar before using. If you don't have either of these cooking tools (and you should!), crush the seeds on a work surface under a heavy saucepan as finely as you can.

white bean soup with garlic and rosemary

MAKES 8 TO 10 SERVINGS

It's a cold winter day, and you need something to warm you and the kids up. Have a bowl of this soup, and you may let them take their sweaters off when they go outside again. This is another bean soup that is so much better when made with dried beans.

1 pound dried white kidney (cannellini) beans

⅓ cup plus 2 tablespoons extra-virgin olive oil

1 large onion, chopped

4 medium carrots, chopped

2 medium celery ribs, chopped

1 large red bell pepper, cored, seeded, and chopped

12 garlic cloves, chopped

2 ripe plum tomatoes, cut into ½-inch dice

1 tablespoon chopped fresh rosemary

1½ teaspoons dried oregano

1 teaspoon hot red pepper flakes

1 gallon water

Kosher salt and freshly ground black pepper to taste

1. At least 8 hours before cooking, place the beans in a large bowl and add enough cold water to cover the beans by 2 inches. Let stand (if the kitchen is warm, refrigerate the bowl of beans) for 8 to 12 hours. (For a quicker alternative, see Note, page 27.) Drain well.

2. Heat the oil in a large pot over medium heat. Add the onion, carrots, celery, bell pepper, and garlic. Cook, stirring often, until the vegetables are softened, about 12 minutes. Add the drained beans, tomatoes, rosemary, oregano, and red pepper flakes and reduce the heat to low. Cook until the tomatoes soften, about 7 minutes. Stir in the water. Bring to a boil over high heat.

3. Reduce the heat to medium-low. Simmer until the beans are very tender, about 1¼ hours. During the last 15 minutes, season with salt and pepper.

4. In batches, transfer the soup to a blender and purée. (Or use a handheld immersion blender to process the soup right in the pot.) Transfer the puréed soup to a bowl. Adjust the seasonings with salt and pepper. Serve hot.

new england fish chowder

MAKES 10 TO 12 SERVINGS

I always make a big pot of this hearty chowder, because even though it's filling, everyone asks for seconds (my daughter Jackie sometimes manages a small bowl for thirds!). The ingredients are very basic, so season it boldly with salt, Worcestershire, and hot pepper sauce. Sea salt provides a slight brininess that I prefer in this soup. For an extra boost of smoky flavor, add about a quarter pound of smoked fish to the chowder along with the fresh fillets.

8 tablespoons (1 stick) unsalted butter

2 large onions, cut lengthwise into quarters, then crosswise into thin slices

1 large leek, white and pale green parts only, thinly sliced and well rinsed

6 garlic cloves, finely chopped

⅔ cup all-purpose flour

2 quarts Fish Stock (see page 43)

¾ pound red-skinned potatoes, scrubbed and each cut into six wedges

2 teaspoons Worcestershire sauce

1 pound fish fillets, such as cod, haddock, pollock, or any firm, white-fleshed fish,
    cut into ¾-inch pieces (see Note, page 29)

1 pint light cream or half-and-half

¼ cup chopped fresh parsley

½ teaspoon hot red pepper sauce, optional

Sea or kosher salt and freshly ground black pepper to taste

1. Melt the butter in a large pot over medium-low heat. Add the onions, leek, and garlic. Cook, stirring often, until the onions are translucent, about 10 minutes. Sprinkle in the flour and mix well. Cook, stirring often, for 3 minutes more, being careful not to let the flour brown. Whisk in the stock and add the potatoes and Worcestershire sauce. Bring to a boil over high heat, stirring often. Reduce the heat to medium-low and simmer until the potatoes are tender, about 25 minutes.

2. Add the fish and cream. Simmer just until the fish turns opaque, about 5 minutes. Remove from the heat and stir in the parsley and hot pepper sauce. Season generously with salt and pepper, and more Worcestershire and hot pepper sauce, if you like. Serve hot.

fish stock

MAKES 2 QUARTS

The only trick to making this stock is finding the fish bones. Happily, most local fish-mongers still fillet whole fish to order, so you should be able to buy frames and heads from these stores. Choose thick-bodied, white-fleshed fish such as sea bass, striped bass, red snapper, or porgy (in fact, a combination is really nice), and skip oily fish like salmon or mackerel.

2 pounds fish frames and/or heads, gills snipped out with sturdy scissors

2 tablespoons vegetable oil

1 large leek, white part only, or 1 large onion, chopped

1 large celery rib, with leaves, chopped

Seasoning Sachet:
 8 fresh parsley sprigs, ½ teaspoon dried thyme, ¼ teaspoon whole black peppercorns, and 1 bay leaf, wrapped in cheesecloth and tied into a bundle

1. Rinse the fish frames and heads well under cold running water to remove any stray viscera.

2. Heat the oil in a large pot over medium heat. Add the leek and celery and cover. Cook, stirring, until softened but not browned, about 5 minutes.

3. Add the fish frames and cover. Cook, stirring occasionally, until the bones begin to give off some juices, about 5 minutes.

4. Add enough cold water to barely cover the bones, about 2 quarts, and add the seasoning sachet. Bring to a boil over high heat, skimming off any foam that rises to the surface. Reduce the heat to low. Simmer, uncovered, for 30 minutes.

5. Strain the stock into a large bowl, and discard the solids. Let stand for 5 minutes and skim the fat from the surface. To store the stock, place the bowl of stock into a larger bowl of ice water and let stand until cool. Cover and refrigerate for up to 3 days, or freeze for up to 2 months.

vegetable broth

MAKES ABOUT 4 QUARTS

Don't settle for water instead of a full-bodied stock in recipes because of pareve cooking restrictions. Use this quick, flavorful vegetable broth instead. The vegetables release their essence very quickly, so you'll have a huge batch of this terrific cooking ingredient in about an hour. Leftovers freeze well for future family suppers.

2 tablespoons vegetable oil

2 large onions, thinly sliced

1 shallot, thinly sliced

5 garlic cloves, minced

1 pound white button mushrooms, quartered

½ pound ripe plum tomatoes, quartered

4 medium carrots, cut into 1-inch pieces

4 medium celery ribs, cut into 1-inch pieces

1 large leek, white part only, split lengthwise into quarters and rinsed

Seasoning Sachet:
    12 parsley sprigs, ½ teaspoon dried thyme, ½ teaspoon whole black peppercorns, and 2 bay leaves, wrapped in cheesecloth and tied into a bundle

1 gallon water

Kosher salt and coarsely ground black pepper to taste

1. Heat the vegetable oil in a large stockpot over medium-high heat. Add the onions, shallot, and garlic and cook just until the onions begin to wilt, about 3 minutes. Stir in the mushrooms, tomatoes, carrots, celery, leek, and sachet. Add 1 gallon water and bring to a boil over high heat.

2. Reduce the heat to low and simmer for 45 to 60 minutes, skimming off any foam that rises to the surface. Season lightly with salt and pepper.

3. Strain into a large bowl and discard the solids. To store the stock, place the bowl in a larger bowl of ice water and let stand until cool. Cover and refrigerate for up to 3 days, or freeze for up to 2 months.

Stocks, Broths, and Bouillon

Although everyone uses the terms interchangeably, there is a difference between stock and broth. Stock is usually made with bones as an ingredient in the recipe; broth has a slightly richer flavor because it is made with meat and bones, and it is seasoned to be consumed as a soup, as well as a recipe ingredient. (The distinction is blurred in the case of vegetable broth, which, of course, is not made with bones or meat.) Homemade stocks have better flavor than anything you can get in a can, box, or cube. I suggest that kosher cooks make their own vegetable broth and fish stock.

They cook quickly, without the same investment of time as chicken or beef stock, and they can be frozen for months.

Every cookbook talks about the value of homemade stock . . . and every cookbook author knows that home cooks rarely make their own stock. There are still options for the busy home cook who wants the taste of full-bodied food. Canned broth, just like anything else, ranges in quality from brand to brand. Heat up some canned broth plain and sip it—if it tastes good, that's the brand for you. At home, we often cook with kosher bouillon powder (sometimes labeled

soup base). I grant that reconstituted bouillon isn't that delicious by itself, but when it is cooked with the other ingredients in the recipe, its flavor improves. I have never found a beef stock product that comes even close to the homemade version, so when using store-bought products, I usually stick to chicken or vegetable broth.

The amount of salt in canned broth and bouillon is an important consideration. When you season the finished dish, taste carefully, as you may need less salt than you expected.

salads

Until recently, the family cook had to commit a fair amount of time to prepare the vegetables for the nightly salad. With the advent of packaged salad greens and the array of prepped vegetables (such as carrots, red cabbage, and coleslaw mix) in bags ready to use, salad can now be made with hardly any prep at all. All it takes is a tasty salad dressing, and this chapter has quite a few of those (see Balsamic-Walnut Vinaigrette, page 56, among others). One word of advice about those prepackaged bags of salad greens. *Prepackaged* does not mean *prewashed,* so rinse well with your vegetable wash (we like the ones with citrus, and not chemical, ingredients), and spin the greens dry before using.

We enjoy salad so much that we make the extra effort to use a variety of vegetables and fruits beyond the typical lettuce-and-tomato fare. Arugula, fennel, hearts of palm, avocado, napa cabbage—these keep our salads interesting. With Jackie or Chad helping, any prep goes very quickly. We joke with each other that we never know what's going to show up in the salad, and that's the way it should be.

Main-course salads, hearty and light at the same time, are one of the healthiest things you can serve for supper. With the addition of some protein (grilled fish, poached or roasted chicken, canned tuna, or sliced steak), many of the side-dish, vegetable salads in this chapter can do double duty as the main event. Where appropriate, I've made suggestions for meat additions to vegetable salads.

asparagus and tofu salad with soy-wasabi vinaigrette

MAKES 4 SERVINGS

Fried tofu is golden, with an irresistibly chewy exterior. If you're pressed for time, use plain tofu, but frying really adds a lot to this salad. With some extra vegetables, such as blanched sugar snap peas or broccoli, this can become a vegetarian main-course salad. Once you have everything prepped, it only takes a few minutes to fry up the tofu, and you're good to go. The instructions here assume that you are serving a chilled salad, but it's also good warm.

Soy-Wasabi Vinaigrette

2 teaspoons soy sauce

1 teaspoon wasabi powder (see Note)

¼ cup unseasoned rice vinegar

¼ teaspoon sugar

¾ cup canola oil

½ teaspoon dark Asian sesame oil

Freshly ground black pepper to taste

One 1-pound package firm tofu, drained

1 pound asparagus, woody ends trimmed

⅓ cup canola oil

1 red bell pepper, cored, seeded, and cut into ¼-inch-wide strips

1 tablespoons sesame seeds, toasted (see page 49)

½ teaspoon black sesame seeds, optional

1. To make the vinaigrette, combine the soy sauce and wasabi in a medium bowl. Whisk in the vinegar and sugar. Gradually whisk in the canola oil, then the sesame oil. Season with the pepper. Cover and refrigerate until ready to serve.

2. Meanwhile, place the tofu on a rimmed plate. Top with another plate and let stand to gently press excess liquid from the tofu, at least 15 minutes and up to 30 minutes. Pat the tofu dry with paper towels and cut into 1-inch cubes.

3. Meanwhile, bring a large saucepan of lightly salted water to a boil over high heat. Add the asparagus and cook just until crisp-tender, about 3 minutes. Drain and rinse under cold running water to stop the cooking. Cut the asparagus spears into thirds. Cover and refrigerate until ready to serve.

4. Line a baking sheet with a double-thickness of paper towels. Heat the oil in a large skillet over high heat until very hot but not smoking. In batches, without crowding, add the tofu cubes and fry, turning occasionally, until they turn golden, about 2 minutes. Add more oil to the skillet as needed. Using a slotted spatula, transfer the fried tofu cubes to the baking sheet.

5. Add the tofu cubes to the vinaigrette and toss with the vinaigrette (the tofu will soak up the dressing, so you need more than for a green salad). Add the asparagus and red pepper and toss again. Use a slotted spoon to transfer equal amounts of the salad to the salad plates. Sprinkle with the toasted sesame seeds, along with the black sesame seeds, if using. Serve immediately.

> **NOTE** Wasabi powder is ground from a hot-tasting root similar to horseradish. When mixed with a small amount of water to make a paste, it turns bright green. For a kosher version, see www.chefjeffgourmet.com, or call 1-888-562-4331.

Sesame Seeds

Toasting sesame seeds really brings out their flavor and it's easy to do. Heat an empty skillet over medium heat until the pan is hot. Add the sesame seeds and cook, stirring often with a wooden spoon, until they are a light tan color. If the seeds start to pop out of the skillet, quickly cover the pan with a lid. Overcooking the sesame seeds will cause them to burn. As soon as they color, turn them out onto a plate to cool.

arugula, fennel, and orange salad

MAKES 6 TO 8 SERVINGS

This salad will perk up the most sluggish appetite. It looks so inviting, with the bright orange sections contrasting with the bright green arugula. In fact, this salad is all about contrast—sweet citrus, aromatic fennel, and mildly bitter arugula. Serve it with grilled sea bass for a main-course salad.

Orange Vinaigrette

¼ cup honey

¼ teaspoon ground fennel seed, optional

Grated zest of 1 orange

¼ cup fresh orange juice

2 tablespoons fresh lemon juice

¾ cup extra-virgin olive oil

Kosher salt and freshly ground black pepper to taste

2 bunches arugula (about ½ pound), trimmed, well rinsed, and dried

½ fennel bulb, thinly sliced crosswise

2 oranges, cut into suprêmes (see page 51)

3 tablespoons pine nuts, toasted (see page 145)

1. To make the vinaigrette, place the honey in a medium bowl and add the fennel seed, if using. Whisk in the zest and orange and lemon juices. Gradually whisk in the oil. Season with salt and pepper.

2. Combine the arugula, fennel, and oranges in a large bowl. Add the vinaigrette and toss well. Sprinkle with the pine nuts. Serve immediately.

Citrus is beloved for its sweet-tart juice and flesh, but thick membranes, bitter seeds, and tough skin must be removed to get to that delicious interior. There is a method of sectioning the fruit into segments without the undesirable parts—the skinless segments are called "suprêmes." Oranges, grapefruit, lemons, and limes can all be prepared in this manner.

Trim the top and bottom off a large seedless orange so that it stands on the work surface. Using a serrated knife, cut off the thick peel where it meets the flesh so you end up with a skinless orange sphere. Working over a medium bowl to catch the juices, hold the orange in one hand and cut between the thin membranes to release the segments, letting them fall into the bowl. Squeeze the juices from the membranes into the bowl. Drain the segments and reserve the juice.

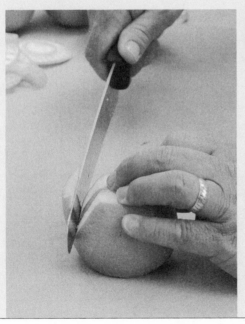 

asian sweet-and-sour slaw

MAKES 4 TO 6 SERVINGS

Coleslaw can be ho-hum, but not in our house. We are always looking for ways to dress up the old favorite. This one, with exotic Asian flavors, is another salad that can do double duty. It is a wonderful side salad (try it instead of the mixed vegetables with the Tilapia Teriyaki on page 134), but may be even better when turned into a hearty main course with lots of shredded cooked chicken or slices of grilled steak.

¼ cup shredded fresh ginger (use the large holes of a box grater)

3 tablespoons unseasoned rice vinegar

2 tablespoons soy sauce

2 teaspoons sugar

1 garlic clove, crushed through a press

½ teaspoon kosher salt, plus more to taste

¼ teaspoon hot red pepper flakes, plus more to taste

½ cup canola oil

1 tablespoon dark Asian sesame oil

6 cups shredded napa cabbage (about 1 pound)

1 large carrot, shredded (about ½ cup)

6 radishes, shredded (about ½ cup)

2 scallions, trimmed, white and green parts, chopped

1. In a medium bowl, combine the ginger, vinegar, soy sauce, sugar, garlic, salt, and red pepper flakes and whisk to combine. Gradually whisk in the canola oil, then the sesame oil.

2. Add the napa cabbage, carrot, radishes, and scallions. Mix well. Season with additional salt and red pepper flakes as needed. Serve immediately. (The slaw can be made up to 1 day ahead, covered, and refrigerated.)

avocado and hearts-of-palm salad with lemon dressing

MAKES 4 TO 6 SERVINGS

Crisp green salad gets a lot of play, but what about a salad of tender, delicious hearts of palm and buttery avocado? If you live in Florida, where it is the state tree, you may know the source of these hearts as the palmetto. It is also called "swamp cabbage," and there is even a "Swamp Cabbage Festival," where I should enter this lemony salad in the annual recipe contest. For the best flavor, use jarred hearts of palm, not canned, which can taste tinny.

One 25-ounce jar hearts of palm, drained and rinsed, cut into ½-inch-thick rounds

2 ripe avocados, pitted, peeled, and diced

2 ripe plum tomatoes, diced

2 tablespoons chopped fresh basil

⅓ cup plus 1 tablespoon fresh lemon juice

½ teaspoon kosher salt, plus more to taste

¼ teaspoon freshly ground black pepper, plus more to taste

½ cup extra-virgin olive oil

½ pound mixed baby greens (mesclun)

1. Combine the hearts of palm, avocados, tomatoes, and basil in a medium bowl.

2. Whisk the lemon juice, salt, and pepper in a small bowl. Gradually whisk in the oil. Pour half of the dressing over the hearts-of-palm mixture and toss gently.

3. Place the mixed greens in a large bowl. Add the remaining dressing and toss well. Season with salt and pepper. Divide equal amounts of the greens on salad plates. Spoon equal amounts of the hearts-of-palm mixture on the greens and top with a grind of fresh pepper. Serve immediately.

poached chicken salad with mustard vinaigrette

MAKES 4 TO 6 SERVINGS

One of the heartiest of main-course salads, it can certainly be made with leftover roasted chicken for a very quick meal. I like to poach the chicken, which also yields a pot of homemade chicken broth to use in other recipes. This is a perfect supper for the dog days of summer, when a cool meal is in order.

Poached Chicken

One 3½-pound chicken, cut into 8 pieces

1 large onion, coarsely chopped

2 medium carrots, coarsely chopped

2 medium celery ribs, coarsely chopped

4 fresh parsley sprigs

¼ teaspoon dried thyme

¼ teaspoon whole black peppercorns

Mustard Vinaigrette

¼ cup red wine vinegar

2 tablespoons fresh lemon juice

2 tablespoons Dijon mustard

1 tablespoon honey

1 garlic clove, crushed under a knife and peeled

½ teaspoon kosher salt

⅔ cup canola oil

1 Belgian endive, cut crosswise into ½-inch-wide strips

1 pint grape or cherry tomatoes, preferably a mix of red and yellow, cut into halves if desired

½ seedless English cucumber, unpeeled, cut into ½-inch dice

½ pound mixed baby greens, such as mesclun

1. To poach the chicken, place the chicken, onion, carrots, and celery in a large saucepan. Add enough cold water to cover by 1 inch. Bring to a boil over high heat, skimming off any foam that rises to the surface. Add the parsley, thyme, and peppercorns. Reduce the heat to medium and simmer until the chicken shows no sign of pink when pierced at the thigh, about 1 hour. Transfer the chicken to a platter and cool until easy to handle. Remove the meat and skin from the bones. Discard the skin and bones, or reserve along with the cooking liquid to use for chicken stock (see Note). Pull apart the meat into thick shreds.

2. To make the vinaigrette, place the vinegar, lemon juice, mustard, honey, garlic, and salt in a blender. With the machine running, add the oil through the hole in the lid.

3. In a medium bowl, mix the chicken, endive, tomatoes, and cucumber with half of the vinaigrette. Toss the greens with the remaining vinaigrette in another bowl. To serve, heap the greens onto dinner plates and top with the chicken salad. Serve immediately.

NOTE To make chicken stock from the poaching liquid: Return the skin and bones to the simmering cooking liquid and simmer for an additional hour. Strain the stock into a bowl. Place the bowl in a larger bowl of ice water and let stand until cool. Skim off the clear fat that rises to the surface of the stock. Pour the stock into covered containers and refrigerate for up to 3 days, or freeze for up to 3 months.

the nathans' house salad

MAKES 4 SERVINGS

Like many families, we use balsamic vinaigrette as our house dressing. A bit of honey plays up the sweetness, and walnut oil gives the dressing a distinctive taste. We keep a jar in the refrigerator to toss with greens as the beginning to the evening's salad. Add whatever other vegetables appeal to you. Actually, you don't have to restrict yourself to vegetables. One of my favorite variations on this salad adds diced dried pears, chopped toasted walnuts, and a topping of crumbled goat cheese.

Balsamic-Walnut Vinaigrette

¼ **cup balsamic vinegar**

1 tablespoon honey

½ **teaspoon kosher salt**

½ **cup extra-virgin olive oil**

¼ **cup walnut oil (see Note)**

Freshly ground black pepper to taste

8 ounces mixed baby greens (mesclun)

1 cup cherry tomatoes

½ **seedless English cucumber, thinly sliced**

1. To make the vinaigrette, whisk the vinegar, honey, and salt in a medium bowl. Gradually whisk in the olive and walnut oils. Season to taste with pepper.

2. Mix the greens, cherry tomatoes, and cucumber in a large bowl. Add the vinaigrette and toss well. Serve immediately.

NOTE Look for light brown walnut oil, not the refined version, as the latter doesn't have nearly as much flavor. Store the oil in the refrigerator. If you can't find it, make a substitute by processing 2 tablespoons chopped walnuts with ¼ cup extra-virgin olive oil in a blender until the walnuts are puréed.

red and yellow israeli salad

MAKES 6 SERVINGS

This classic Mediterranean salad is usually served with heaps of hot pita bread as a light appetizer, but it is much more than a side dish. Top it with grilled fish fillets or poached chicken, and you have a meal. If you don't have yellow tomatoes, substitute about 8 more plum tomatoes. And, as the salad looks best when all of the vegetables are the same size, take some time to cut the vegetables into uniform cubes about $1/2$-inch square.

2 tablespoons fresh lemon juice

1 teaspoon sugar

$1/4$ cup extra-virgin olive oil

4 ripe plum tomatoes, seeded and chopped

2 ripe yellow tomatoes, chopped

1 seedless English cucumber, unpeeled, chopped

1 red bell pepper, cored, seeded, and chopped

1 green bell pepper, cored, seeded, and chopped

$1/3$ cup chopped fresh mint or basil

Kosher salt and freshly ground black pepper to taste

1. Whisk the lemon juice and sugar in a large bowl. Gradually whisk in the oil. Add the plum and yellow tomatoes, cucumber, bell peppers, and mint, and mix gently to combine. Season with salt and pepper.

2. Cover and refrigerate at least 1 hour and up to 4 hours. Serve chilled.

caribbean macaroni salad

MAKES 8 TO 10 SERVINGS

This is another salad that shows up often at our family cookouts. The secret ingredient is sweetened cream of coconut (don't confuse it with coconut milk!), one of the essentials of the ever-popular piña colada. You'll find it in the supermarket's Latino section, in the aisle with the mixers for alcoholic beverages, or in liquor stores. Be sure to stir it well before using—shaking the can doesn't do it. Refrigerate leftovers in a covered container for a week or so, and plan to make a blender of piña coladas or smoothies to use it up.

1 pound elbow macaroni

½ cup canned pineapple juice

2 tablespoons curry powder

2 cups mayonnaise

1 soft-ripe medium banana, mashed

¼ cup sweetened cream of coconut, such as Coco Lopez

2 tablespoons fresh lime juice

½ teaspoon hot red pepper sauce

¼ teaspoon freshly ground black pepper

1 cup (¼-inch dice) green bell pepper

1 cup (¼-inch dice) red bell pepper

3 scallions, finely chopped

Kosher salt to taste

1. Bring a large pot of lightly salted water to a boil over high heat. Add the macaroni and cook until tender, about 9 minutes. Drain, and rinse well under cold running water. Drain again. Transfer to a large bowl.

2. Stir the pineapple juice and curry powder in a medium bowl to evenly disperse the curry powder. Add the mayonnaise, banana, cream of coconut, lime juice, hot sauce, and black pepper and mix until smooth. Fold in the green and red bell peppers and scallions. Add to the macaroni and mix well. Season with salt.

3. Cover and refrigerate until well chilled, about 2 hours. Serve chilled.

ali's italian potato salad

MAKES 8 TO 10 SERVINGS

This potato salad makes an appearance at almost every Nathan family barbecue, made by Ali in proportions that have never been written down until now. We love it freshly made and served warm or at room temperature. However, we have not been known to turn down the chilled leftovers, either.

3 pounds red-skinned potatoes, scrubbed but unpeeled

1½ cups mayonnaise

⅓ cup balsamic vinegar

1 small red onion, finely chopped

4 celery ribs, finely chopped

¾ teaspoon celery seed

1 teaspoon freshly ground black pepper, plus more to taste

½ teaspoon kosher salt, plus more to taste

1. Place the potatoes in a large pot of lightly salted water and bring to a boil over high heat. Cook until tender when pierced with the tip of a knife, about 25 minutes. Drain and cool until easy to handle. Cut the unpeeled potatoes into quarters or smaller, depending on their size, and return to the cooking pot.

2. Mix the mayonnaise, balsamic vinegar, onion, and celery in a small bowl. Add the celery seed, pepper, and salt and mix again. Add to the warm potatoes and mix gently, trying not to break up the potatoes. Taste and adjust the seasoning with salt and pepper. Serve warm or cooled to room temperature. If held at room temperature for more than 2 hours after making, refrigerate.

mexican chopped salad with toasted cumin vinaigrette

MAKES 6 TO 8 SERVINGS

The hearty beans make this an option for a vegetarian main-course salad. Chopped apples add a sweet, crunchy element of surprise to the salad. If you want to add a protein, roasted chicken is a great meat option, but sliced grilled steak would be good, too. The dressing purposely makes extra for leftovers to serve with another meal.

Cumin Vinaigrette

¼ cup cider vinegar

2½ tablespoons honey

2 tablespoons fresh lime juice

1½ tablespoons soy sauce

2 teaspoons ground cumin (see Note)

½ teaspoon chili powder

1 large garlic clove, crushed under a knife and peeled

1 cup canola oil

2 tablespoons chopped fresh cilantro

Kosher salt and freshly ground black pepper to taste

2 cups fresh or thawed frozen corn kernels

One 15- to 19-ounce can black beans, drained and rinsed

One 14-ounce can roasted red peppers, drained and chopped

5 ripe plum tomatoes, chopped

2 Red Delicious apples, cored and chopped

1 head romaine lettuce, cut crosswise into ½-inch strips, then coarsely chopped

1. To make the cumin vinaigrette, put the vinegar, honey, lime juice, soy sauce, cumin, chili powder, and garlic in a blender. With the machine running, add the oil through the hole in the lid. Add the cilantro and pulse to blend. Season with salt and pepper. Set aside.

2. Mix the corn, beans, red peppers, tomatoes, and apples in a large bowl. Add the lettuce strips and toss. Add as much vinaigrette as desired, saving the leftover vinaigrette for another use. Mix well and serve immediately.

NOTE If you have time, freshly toasted ground whole cumin seeds will add a lot of extra flavor to this vinaigrette. Heat a small empty skillet over medium heat. Add 2 teaspoons cumin seeds and stir occasionally until lightly toasted (you will be able to smell them, and you may see a wisp of smoke), about 2 minutes. Transfer to a plate and cool completely. Grind in a spice grinder or electric coffee grinder.

House Salad Dressing

While the salad dressings in this book were designed to be components of particular salads, many of them work on their own as individual dressings, ready to be tossed with your favorite greens and other salad vegetables.

Rather than making just enough dressing for tonight's salad, get in the habit of making a double or even triple batch. Transfer the leftover dressing to a covered container and refrigerate, where it will keep for at least a week. The dressing will usually separate, but it will come back together when whisked or shaken (be sure the lid on the container is tight).

In families where not everyone has the same taste, it's not difficult to have two or three different dressings in the refrigerator, allowing everyone to exercise their personal taste. For variety, you might want to make contrasting dressings, such as the slightly sweet Orange Vinaigrette and the thick, creamy Garbanzo Vinaigrette.

Here are the individual salad dressings in the book. One of them is bound to become your house dressing.

Soy-Wasabi Vinaigrette (page 48)

Orange Vinaigrette (page 50)

Mustard Vinaigrette (page 54)

Balsamic-Walnut Vinaigrette (page 56)

Cumin Vinaigrette (page 60)

Mushroom Vinaigrette (page 63)

Garbanzo Vinaigrette (page 64)

pasta salad niçoise

MAKES 4 TO 6 SERVINGS

This cold salad fills the usual requirements for the genre, being perfectly suited to warm-weather family get-togethers. But, this one can also be packed into the kids' lunch boxes. Don't underestimate the sophistication of your kids' palates. Because pasta salad has a tendency to lose its piquancy as it stands, you might want to pack along a lemon wedge too, as a squeeze of fresh juice will wake the salad up.

½ pound baby shell-shaped pasta

¼ cup fresh lemon juice, plus more as needed

1 garlic clove, crushed through a press

1 teaspoon kosher salt, plus more to taste

½ teaspoon freshly ground black pepper, plus more to taste

½ cup extra-virgin olive oil

Two 6-ounce cans white tuna in water, drained

2 ripe plum tomatoes, chopped

½ cup chopped (½-inch dice) seedless English cucumber

¼ cup finely chopped red onion

¼ cup chopped fresh basil

¼ cup pitted and chopped black Mediterranean olives

1. Bring a large pot of lightly salted water to a boil over high heat. Add the pasta and cook until tender, about 9 minutes. Drain, rinse under cold running water, and drain well.

2. Whisk the lemon juice, garlic, salt, and pepper in a medium bowl. Gradually whisk in the oil.

3. Add the pasta, tuna, tomatoes, cucumber, red onion, basil, and olives and toss gently. Season with additional salt and pepper as needed. Cover and refrigerate until chilled, at least 2 hours or overnight.

4. Just before serving, taste and add more lemon juice, salt, and pepper as needed. Serve chilled.

baby spinach salad with warm mushroom vinaigrette

MAKES 6 SERVINGS

Remember the days when a fresh spinach salad meant trimming and washing piles of leaves? Well, those days are over, thanks to the bags of baby spinach widely available in the market today. The spinach should get a quick rinse and spin just to be sure that it's good and clean, but that's still much easier than washing in several changes of water to remove grit. It makes a sophisticated recipe like this one, with its warm topping of sautéed mushrooms, simple enough to make for a family supper.

Mushroom Vinaigrette

⅓ **cup plus 2 tablespoons extra-virgin olive oil**

1 medium red onion, halved lengthwise and thinly sliced into half-moons

4 garlic cloves, smashed under a knife and peeled

10 ounces cremini mushrooms, thinly sliced

2 tablespoons fresh lemon juice

2 tablespoons balsamic vinegar

½ **teaspoon sugar**

Kosher salt and freshly ground black pepper to taste

9 ounces baby spinach

½ **pint grape or cherry tomatoes, halved**

1. To make the vinaigrette, combine ⅓ cup of the oil, half of the red onion, and the garlic in a large skillet over medium-low heat. Cover and cook until the onion is crisp-tender, about 5 minutes. Stir in the mushrooms, cover, and cook until they give off their juices, about 5 minutes more. Stir in the lemon juice, balsamic vinegar, and sugar. Season with the salt and pepper. Remove from the heat and stir in the remaining red onion and 2 tablespoons olive oil.

2. Toss the spinach and cherry tomatoes in a large bowl. Pour the mushroom dressing on top and toss again. Serve immediately.

romaine salad with garbanzo vinaigrette

MAKES 6 SERVINGS

Fans of full-bodied salad dressings will appreciate this thick and tangy vinaigrette. It needs a sturdy lettuce to stand up to its heft, so romaine is the best choice. Any left-over dressing will keep for about ten days, tightly covered, in the refrigerator. If you want to add some protein to this salad, try canned or grilled tuna.

Garbanzo Vinaigrette

$\frac{1}{2}$ cup drained canned garbanzo beans (chickpeas), rinsed
(about half of a drained 19-ounce can)

1 ripe plum tomato, quartered

2 garlic cloves, crushed under a knife and peeled

3 tablespoons fresh lemon juice

$2\frac{1}{2}$ tablespoons balsamic vinegar

1 teaspoon Dijon mustard

1 teaspoon chopped fresh thyme or $\frac{1}{2}$ teaspoon dried thyme

$1\frac{1}{2}$ teaspoons kosher salt

$\frac{1}{2}$ teaspoon freshly ground black pepper

1 cup olive oil

1 large head romaine lettuce, cut into 1- to 2-inch pieces

$\frac{1}{2}$ cup drained canned garbanzo beans (chickpeas), rinsed
(about half of a drained 19-ounce can)

4 ripe plum tomatoes, cut into $\frac{1}{2}$-inch dice

1 cup store-bought croutons

1. To make the vinaigrette, combine the garbanzo beans, tomato, and garlic in a blender or food processor. Add $3\frac{1}{2}$ tablespoons water, the lemon juice, balsamic vinegar, mustard, thyme, salt, and pepper. With the machine running, gradually add the oil through the hole in the blender lid or the feed tube of the processor, and blend to make a thick dressing. Transfer to a serving bowl.

2. Toss the lettuce, chickpeas, tomatoes, and croutons in a large bowl. Serve the salad, passing the vinaigrette on the side.

DAIRY VARIATION

Add 3 ounces feta cheese, coarsely crumbled, to the salad.

chicken and turkey

Week in and week out, cooking poultry remains a favorite way to get supper on the table, but that doesn't mean it has to be mundane. We serve chicken and turkey grilled on salad greens, roasted to perfection, fragrant with spices, tangy with sweet-and-sour sauce . . . just about any way it can be cooked.

When kids come into the equation for supper menu planning, there is one surefire hit—crunchy chicken. I offer three recipes here: one fragrant with African-style spices for the more adventuresome diners in the family; chicken breast strips crusted with matzo for the conservatives; and another with a thick oregano-scented coating for the middle-of-the-road diners. To say that these are a lot better than the crunchy strips kids would order at a fast-food joint is a huge understatement.

Boneless, skinless chicken breast has become mainstream in today's kitchens—it cooks quickly, is extremely versatile, and goes well with different flavors. On the other hand, it is easy to overcook, and many of us are familiar with the tough texture of chicken breast that has stayed too long on the fire. The brine in the koshering process does add some moisture to the breasts, but that doesn't mean that you can be careless about cooking them. Allow about 12 minutes to cook whole chicken breasts in a skillet over medium heat, and less (about 6 minutes) if using cutlets, or if the breast is cut into pieces. One way to test for doneness is to press the center of the cooked breast with your finger—it should feel just firm enough to spring back to your touch. Get away from the habit of piercing the breast with the tip of a knife to check the interior color, as that is a sure way to lose precious juices.

fried chicken breasts with african spices

MAKES 4 SERVINGS

Fried chicken does not necessarily mean it must be Southern-fried, and this version gives some kick to the old family supper standby. I learned to appreciate the spicy flavors of North Africa when I was in the Navy. Wherever I went, from Morocco to Yemen, the seasonings knocked me out. The crust of this chicken is perfectly seasoned, so you won't need more than a squeeze of lemon juice as a condiment. But, if you want to make it fancier, serve it with Zhug Mayonnaise (page 132) as a dip, or with a drizzle of Cumin Vinaigrette (page 60). As good as the spices are, it is the panko that makes the crust extra-special. If you aren't familiar with this terrific ingredient, pick up a couple of bags—you won't regret it.

If there are picky eaters in your family who don't like spices, no problem, simply make a half batch of the coating with the spices, leave the spices out of the other half, and increase the amount of panko by a quarter cup. Plain couscous and steamed baby-cut carrots would be nice side dishes.

2 cups panko (flaky Japanese bread crumbs, see Note)

1 tablespoon ground ginger

**1 tablespoon ground fennel seed
(see page 39)**

1 tablespoon ground cumin

1 tablespoon ground coriander

1 teaspoon ground allspice

1 teaspoon ground cinnamon

1 teaspoon freshly ground black pepper

½ cup all-purpose flour

3 large eggs

Four 7-ounce boneless, skinless chicken breasts

⅓ cup extra-virgin olive oil

Lemon wedges, for serving

1. Mix the panko, ginger, fennel, cumin, coriander, allspice, cinnamon, and pepper in a shallow dish. Place the flour in another shallow dish. Beat the eggs and 2 tablespoons water in a third shallow dish.

2. One at a time, dip the chicken breasts in the flour and shake off the excess. Dip in the eggs, then in the panko mixture to coat, gently pressing the panko coating to adhere. Place on a baking sheet and refrigerate for 15 minutes to set the crust.

3. Position a rack in the center of the oven and preheat the oven to 375°F. Heat the oil in a very large skillet over medium-high heat until very hot but not smoking. Add the chicken breasts to the skillet. Cook, turning once, until the crust is golden brown, about 4 minutes. Transfer the breasts to a baking sheet. Bake until the chicken feels firm when pressed in the center, 10 to 12 minutes.

4. Transfer the chicken to paper towels to drain briefly. Serve hot with the lemon wedges.

NOTE Panko is crisp Japanese bread crumbs and great for coating fried foods. It is available at Asian grocers and many supermarkets. A kosher version is available through Chef Jeff Gourmet, www.chefjeffgourmet.com, 1-888-562-4331.

chicken with broccoli and lemon sauce

MAKES 6 SERVINGS

I bet that the second time you make this chicken-and-veggies sauté, you'll be able to get dinner on the table in under fifteen minutes. And I also wager that it will become a family favorite, especially for the cook, who can easily change the vegetables to accommodate the whims of the diners. I've made it with previously cooked asparagus, red peppers, and scallions, all with great success. And I am happy to use individually frozen broccoli florets as a time saver. Be sure to use a large skillet so everything will fit in the pan at once.

Six 7-ounce boneless and skinless chicken breasts, each cut into 4 pieces

1 teaspoon dried oregano

¾ teaspoon freshly ground black pepper

½ cup all-purpose flour

¼ cup olive oil

2 small red onions, halved lengthwise and thinly sliced into half-moons

6 garlic cloves, thinly sliced

½ cup dry white wine

½ cup fresh lemon juice

Grated zest of 2 lemons

3 cups thawed frozen broccoli florets

1 cup chicken broth

1 tablespoon cornstarch

Kosher salt to taste

1. Season the chicken with the oregano and pepper. Dip each piece in flour and shake to remove the excess.

2. Heat the oil in a large skillet over medium-high heat. Add the chicken (do this in batches if the skillet isn't large enough to cook the chicken without crowding), and cook until the undersides are browned, about 3 minutes. Turn the chicken, and add the red onions, moving the chicken so the majority of onions touch the bottom of the skillet. Cook until the onions soften, about 6 minutes.

3. Use a wooden spatula to scrape up any browned bits in the bottom of the pan. Use the spatula to clear a space in the skillet, and fill the space with the garlic. Cook until the garlic softens, about 2 minutes. Add the wine and lemon juice and zest and stir up any new browned bits from the bottom of the skillet. Scatter the broccoli on top of the chicken, pour in ¾ cup broth, and cover tightly. Reduce the heat to medium-low and simmer until the broccoli is heated through, about 3 minutes.

4. Pour the remaining ¼ cup of broth into a small bowl. Add the cornstarch and mix until dissolved. Add the cornstach mixture to the skillet and cook until the sauce returns to a simmer and thickens, about 1 minute. Season the sauce with salt and pepper. Serve hot.

Cooking with Your Kids

Recently, one of my cooking students came up to me after a class. He said that he had a problem. He had to cook two dinners every night, one for himself and his wife, and another for his kids, who were such picky eaters they didn't want anything more than pasta with cheese on a regular basis.

I asked him if he ever cooked with his kids. He looked surprised, with a "why would I want to do such a thing?" expression. I explained that if his kids felt that they were making something special for the family to share, maybe they would be tempted into eating their creations. I also went through my list of reasons why kids should spend plenty of time in the kitchen.

- It's more educational than 99 percent of TV, providing math skills, lessons in hygiene and cultural studies, and nutritional information, all while making something delicious.
- It gives the family time for hanging out and talking—in a casual setting, it is interesting what youngsters will reveal.
- Cooking improves motor skills in younger kids (start off with easy stuff like popping stems from mushrooms, then move on to snipping herbs; eventually try them on the big projects, such as chopping with a knife).
- This experience provides a touchstone for maturity (my teenager Chad has discovered how many girls are impressed by a man-cooked meal, and young Jackie loves to collect family recipes and their histories).

He had to admit that it sounded reasonable, and he promised to get back to me with a follow-up report.

The next time I saw him, he came up and shook my hand. He said that the kids loved being a part of the dinner-making process, and now came to Dad with suggestions of things to cook. The family had even sat down to a few meals where everyone ate the same thing, which was a vast improvement. He said that the kids hadn't asked to attend the Culinary Institute of America yet, but there was plenty of time for that!

matzo-crusted chicken strips with honey-mustard dip

MAKES 4 TO 6 SERVINGS

This is one heck of a kid-friendly supper. Chicken tenders are sometimes hard to find in kosher butchers, but there's nothing to stop you from cutting breasts into strips. With three kinds of matzo products, the strips have the perfect amount of crunch; a two-stage cooking method keeps the matzo from burning during frying.

Honey-Mustard Dip

$\frac{1}{2}$ cup Dijon mustard (use kosher for Passover mustard during the holiday)

$\frac{1}{4}$ cup honey

1 teaspoon chopped fresh rosemary

$\frac{1}{4}$ teaspoon freshly ground black pepper

Matzo Crust

$\frac{2}{3}$ cup matzo meal

$\frac{2}{3}$ cup matzo farfel

$\frac{2}{3}$ cup matzo flour

2 tablespoons chopped fresh parsley

2 tablespoons chopped fresh basil or 1 tablespoon chopped fresh rosemary or thyme

2 pounds skinless and boneless chicken breast

$\frac{1}{2}$ teaspoon freshly ground black pepper

$\frac{1}{2}$ cup matzo flour

3 large eggs

Extra-virgin olive oil, for frying

1. Position a rack in the center of the oven and preheat to 350°F.

2. To make the mustard dip, mix the mustard, honey, rosemary, and pepper in a small bowl. Cover and set aside.

3. To make the matzo crust, mix the matzo meal, matzo farfel, matzo flour, parsley, and basil in a shallow dish. Set aside.

4. Cut the chicken breasts lengthwise into 2 or 3 pieces. Season the chicken strips with pepper.

5. Place the matzo flour in a shallow dish. Beat the eggs in a medium bowl with 2 tablespoons water. A few strips at a time, dredge the chicken in the plain matzo flour and shake off the excess. Dip the strips in the egg wash and coat with the matzo crust mixture. Place the breaded chicken strips on a baking sheet.

6. Pour enough oil into a large skillet to come about $\frac{1}{4}$ inch up the sides. Heat the oil over medium-high heat until very hot but not smoking. In batches, without crowding, add the chicken to the skillet and fry until golden brown, about 4 minutes. Using a slotted spatula, transfer the browned strips to another baking sheet, spreading them apart.

7. Bake until the chicken is cooked through, 8 to 10 minutes. Serve hot with the dip.

grilled chicken on mixed greens with mango salsa

MAKES 4 SERVINGS

Whenever I eat this dish, I feel like I've jumped out of the pages of a healthy living magazine. You've got a brightly colored, vibrantly flavored salsa, served with lean grilled chicken on a heap of greens, and not a drop of oil in sight!

Mango Salsa

2 ripe mangoes, pitted, peeled, and cut into thin matchsticks

1 small red bell pepper, cored, seeded, and cut into thin matchsticks

1 small green bell pepper, cored, seeded, and cut into thin matchsticks

3 tablespoons chopped fresh cilantro

½ jalapeño, seeds and ribs removed, finely chopped

¼ cup fresh lime juice

Kosher salt and freshly ground black pepper to taste

Four 7-ounce skinless, boneless chicken breasts

¼ teaspoon freshly ground black pepper

8 ounces mixed baby greens (mesclun)

Lime wedges, for serving

1. To make the salsa, combine all of the salsa ingredients and season with the salt and pepper. Cover and refrigerate for at least 2 hours and up to 8 hours.

2. Build a charcoal fire on one side of an outdoor grill and let burn until the coals are covered with white ash. For a gas grill, preheat on high. Keep one burner on high, and turn the other burner to low. Lightly oil the grill grate. Lightly season the breasts with pepper. Place the breasts over the coals (or on the high burner of the gas grill) and cover the grill. Cook until sear marks form on the undersides of the breasts, about 2 minutes. Turn and repeat on the other side, about 2 minutes. Move the chicken to the side of the grill without the coals (or to the low burner on the gas grill) and cover the grill. Continue cooking until the chicken feels firm when pressed in the thickest part, about 12 minutes.

3. Heap equal amounts of the salad on four dinner plates. Top each with a chicken breast, then a large spoonful of the salsa. Serve immediately with the lime wedges.

chicken and mushroom fricassee

MAKES 4 TO 6 SERVINGS

This creamy, saucy dish (without any cream, of course) is made to be spooned over mashed potatoes. Use as many different mushrooms as you can to give the most interesting flavor (see page 35).

⅓ cup vegetable oil, such as canola

10 thin-sliced chicken cutlets

Freshly ground black pepper to taste

¾ cup sliced shallots (about 3 large shallots)

6 garlic cloves, finely chopped

1½ pounds assorted fresh mushrooms, cut into quarters

¼ cup all-purpose flour

2 cups chicken broth

1 cup dry white wine, such as Chardonnay

3 tablespoons chopped fresh herbs, such as parsley, rosemary, and basil, in any combination

Kosher salt to taste

Hot cooked egg noodles, for serving

1. Heat the oil in a large skillet over medium-high heat. Season the chicken with pepper. In batches, without crowding, add the chicken to the skillet and cook, turning once, until lightly browned on both sides, about 4 minutes. Transfer the browned chicken to a plate.

2. Return all of the browned chicken to the skillet. Add the shallots and garlic, being sure they touch the bottom of the skillet, and cook for 1 minute. Add the mushrooms and cook until they release their liquid and are beginning to brown, about 10 minutes. Sprinkle with the flour and stir well. Cook, stirring often, for 1 minute, adjusting the heat as needed to ensure that the flour doesn't brown. Add the broth and wine, stirring to release the browned bits in the pan. Bring to a simmer.

3. Reduce the heat to medium-low and simmer until the chicken is cooked through, about 15 minutes. Stir in the herbs and season the sauce with salt and pepper. Serve hot, on the noodles.

chicken legs with spicy honey glaze

MAKES 4 TO 6 SERVINGS

You've heard of finger-lickin' good chicken? Well, this chicken, with a sweet-and-sour glaze and dip made from the same few ingredients, will give that chicken adage a run for its money. For a simple side dish, toss red potatoes (cut into 1-inch chunks) and carrots (cut into 2-inch lengths) with olive oil, season with salt and pepper, and spread on a baking sheet. Roast these vegetables on another oven rack along with the chicken. If you want to use dried thyme instead of fresh, add 1 teaspoon to the marinade and $1/8$ teaspoon to the sauce.

1 cup honey

$1/2$ cup cider vinegar

2 tablespoons chopped fresh thyme

$1\frac{1}{8}$ teaspoons hot red pepper flakes

$1/4$ teaspoon kosher salt, plus more to taste

6 chicken drumsticks

6 chicken thighs

1 tablespoon cornstarch

Freshly ground black pepper to taste

1. To make a marinade, mix $1/2$ cup honey, $1/4$ cup vinegar, 1 tablespoon thyme, 1 teaspoon red pepper flakes, and $1/4$ teaspoon kosher salt in a large zippered plastic bag. Add the chicken and marinate at room temperature for 30 minutes to 1 hour.

2. Meanwhile, position a rack in the center of the oven and preheat the oven to 400°F. Line a roasting pan with aluminum foil and lightly oil the foil.

3. Arrange the chicken in the roasting pan, and pour the marinade on top. Roast, basting occasionally with the marinade, until the chicken shows no sign of pink when pierced at a bone, about 50 minutes.

4. Meanwhile, in a medium saucepan bring the remaining $1/2$ cup honey, $1/4$ cup vinegar, 1 tablespoon thyme, and $1/8$ teaspoon red pepper flakes to a simmer over medium heat, whisking constantly. It will foam up, so be sure the saucepan is large enough. Reduce the heat to low.

5. Pour 2 tablespoons cold water in a small bowl, add the cornstarch, and whisk to dissolve. Whisk the cornstarch mixture into the simmering sauce—the sauce will become quite thick. Set aside.

6. Transfer the chicken to a serving platter. Whisk 1 or 2 tablespoons of the baking juices into the sauce to thin it to dipping consistency. Season the sauce with pepper. Drizzle the sauce over the chicken, or pour it into a small bowl and serve on the side, as a dipping sauce. Serve hot.

smothered chicken with onions and jalapeño

MAKES 4 SERVINGS

In a way, this is a kind of chicken chili, but even better. The onions, garlic, and jalapeño almost melt into a sauce, and the quartet of ingredients in the spice rub will fill your kitchen with the kind of aromas that cookbook authors love to write about and families love to smell. Serve this with Orzo and Garbanzos (page 199) to soak up the juices.

¼ cup onion powder

3 tablespoons garlic powder

3 tablespoons dried oregano

1 tablespoon ground ancho chile (see Note, page 99) or chili powder

1 tablespoon kosher salt

1 teaspoon freshly ground black pepper

8 chicken leg quarters

½ cup extra-virgin olive oil

⅓ cup chopped fresh cilantro

6 garlic cloves, minced

1 jalapeño, sliced into thin rings, seeds included

3 medium onions, halved lengthwise and thinly sliced into half-moons

1. Position a rack in the center of the oven and preheat the oven to 400°F. Mix the onion and garlic powders, oregano, ground chile, salt, and pepper together.

2. Place the chicken in a roasting pan. Drizzle with the oil and sprinkle with the cilantro and garlic. Mix well with your hands. Sprinkle with the spice mixture and mix again. Top with the sliced jalapeño and onions. Pour 1 cup water in the bottom of the pan.

3. Roast, adding more water, if needed, to keep the spices from scorching in the pan, until the chicken shows no sign of pink when pierced at the thighbone, about 45 minutes. Serve hot.

baked chicken breasts oreganata

MAKES 4 SERVINGS

This is another Nathan family favorite, chicken breasts baked with a thick crust of Italian herbs and garlic. Keep the side dishes simple so the herbs in the crust can shine. How about the Red and Yellow Israeli Salad (page 57)?

Oregano Crust

1 cup Italian-seasoned dried bread crumbs

8 garlic cloves, minced

¼ cup finely chopped fresh parsley

2 teaspoons dried oregano

1 teaspoon dried basil

½ teaspoon kosher salt

½ teaspoon freshly ground black pepper

⅓ cup extra-virgin olive oil, as needed

Four 6-ounce boneless, skinless chicken breasts

¼ cup dry white wine, such as Chardonnay, or chicken broth or water

3 tablespoons extra-virgin olive oil

2 tablespoons fresh lemon juice

Lemon wedges, for serving

1. Position a rack in the top third of the oven and preheat the oven to 400°F. Lightly oil a 13 × 9-inch baking dish.

2. To make the oregano crust, mix the bread crumbs, garlic, parsley, oregano, basil, salt, and pepper in a small bowl. Stir in enough olive oil to give the mixture the consistency of wet sand.

3. Place the chicken breasts in the baking dish. Pat equal amounts of the oregano crust in a thick, even layer on top of each breast. Pour the wine, oil, and lemon juice around the chicken. Bake until the top is golden brown and the chicken shows no sign of pink when pierced with the tip of a sharp knife, about 20 minutes.

4. Serve the chicken breasts hot with lemon wedges.

chicken stir-fry with pineapple, peanuts, and jalapeño

MAKES 4 TO 6 SERVINGS

You certainly are going to want to serve rice with this dish to absorb every last drop of the spicy-sweet sauce! Steamed broccoli florets would be perfect on the side. This stir-fry can be ready in about the time it takes for the rice to cook.

One 20-ounce can pineapple chunks in juice

4 boneless, skinless chicken cutlets, each cut in half and lightly pounded

½ teaspoon freshly ground black pepper

½ cup all-purpose flour

4 tablespoons canola oil

2 medium onions, cut into thin half-moons

1 red bell pepper, cored, seeded, and cut into thin strips

1 jalapeño, seeded and minced

2 teaspoons minced fresh ginger

3 garlic cloves, chopped

1 cup chicken broth

¼ cup fresh lime juice

½ cup unsalted roasted peanuts or cashews

2 teaspoons cornstarch

1. Drain the pineapple in a sieve over a bowl, reserve the chunks, and measure the juices. You need ½ cup plus 2 tablespoons pineapple juice. If necessary, add water to the juice to make up the difference.

2. Season the chicken with the pepper. Spread the flour on a plate. Dip the chicken on both sides in the flour and shake off the excess.

3. Heat 2 tablespoons of the oil in a large nonstick skillet over medium-high heat. In batches, without crowding, add the chicken and cook until browned on both sides, about 5 minutes. Transfer to a plate.

4. Add the remaining 2 tablespoons oil to the skillet. Add the onions, bell pepper, jalapeño, ginger, and garlic and stir-fry until the onions are translucent, about 5 minutes. Stir in the chicken broth, lime juice, and ½ cup of the pineapple juice. Return the chicken to the skillet and reduce the heat to medium-low. Cook, turning the chicken occasionally, until it looks opaque when pierced with the tip of a knife, about 5 minutes. Using a slotted spoon, transfer the chicken to a platter.

5. Add the pineapple chunks and peanuts to the skillet. Pour the remaining 2 tablespoons pineapple juice into a small bowl, add the cornstarch, and stir to dissolve. Whisk the cornstarch mixture into the skillet and cook until the sauce is thickened and the pineapple is cooked through, about 1 minute. Pour the vegetables and sauce over the chicken and serve hot.

chicken in sweet-and-sour sauce

MAKES 4 SERVINGS

If all Chinese takeout was as fresh-tasting as this, I'd order out all the time. Making sweet-and-sour chicken at home allows me to make it to my own taste, which means loading it up with lots of Asian greens for added nutrition and flavor. In fact, we like sweet-and-sour dishes so much that we make a double batch of the sauce to keep in the refrigerator (it keeps for at least three weeks) for other meals. Try it as a dip for the Spicy Batter-Fried Tilapia on page 132.

Sweet-and-Sour Sauce

½ **cup sugar**

½ **cup water**

⅓ **cup plus 1 tablespoon rice wine vinegar**

1 **tablespoon ketchup**

1 **tablespoon soy sauce**

1 **tablespoon peeled and finely chopped fresh ginger**

3 **garlic cloves, finely chopped**

½ **of a star anise, about 4 points, optional**

1 **tablespoon cornstarch**

⅔ **cup cornstarch, as needed**

⅓ **cup canola oil, or more as needed**

Six 7-ounce boneless, skinless chicken breasts, each cut into 3 pieces

1 **tablespoon finely chopped fresh ginger**

1 **garlic clove, finely chopped**

1½ **cups packed coarsely chopped napa cabbage**

1 **cup packed coarsely chopped bok choy**

1 **medium red bell pepper, cored, seeded, and diced**

1 **teaspoon dark Asian sesame oil**

Hot cooked rice, for serving

1. To make the sweet-and-sour sauce, bring the sugar, water, rice vinegar, ketchup, soy sauce, ginger, garlic, and star anise, if using, to a boil in a small saucepan over medium heat, stirring often. Reduce the heat to low and simmer to blend the flavors, about 3 minutes.

2. Sprinkle the 1 tablespoon cornstarch over 2 tablespoons water in a small bowl and stir with a fork to dissolve. Whisk the cornstarch mixture into the simmering sauce and cook to thicken, about 1 minute. Remove from the heat. If using the star anise, remove it from the sauce.

3. For the rest of the dish, spread the $\frac{2}{3}$ cup cornstarch in a shallow dish. Heat the oil in a very large skillet over medium-high heat until very hot but not smoking. Coat the chicken in the cornstarch and shake off the excess. Add the chicken to the skillet, working in batches if necessary. Cook, turning once, until golden brown, about 3 minutes. Transfer the chicken to a plate.

4. Add more oil to the skillet, if needed, and heat. Add the ginger and garlic to the skillet and cook until the garlic gives off its aroma, about 1 minute. Add the cabbage, bok choy, and bell pepper and mix well. Return the chicken to the skillet. Reduce the heat to low and simmer until the chicken is cooked through, about 10 minutes. Stir in the sweet-and-sour sauce and bring to a simmer. Remove from the heat and stir in the sesame oil. Serve hot, with the rice.

twice-cooked chicken with tomatoes and cumin

MAKES 4 SERVINGS

The incredible aromas of this dish will act like a dinner bell to gather the family into the kitchen and around the dinner table. To get a deeply colored skin and evenly cooked flesh, the chicken is first seared in the skillet to encourage tasty surface browning, then popped in the oven with the other ingredients to create a spicy sauce. Buy a chicken that is on the small side, as large birds take so long to cook that the sauce may scorch. You'll want to serve this with Hummus and Roasted Garlic Mashed Potatoes (page 203) or simple steamed rice to soak it all up.

¼ **cup olive oil**

One 3½-pound chicken, cut into 8 serving pieces

½ **cup all-purpose flour**

1 large red onion, chopped

6 garlic cloves, minced

1 jalapeño, seeded and minced

1 teaspoon ground turmeric

1 teaspoon ground cumin

One 28-ounce can chopped tomatoes in juice

1 cup chicken broth

Grated zest of 1 lemon

1. Position a rack in the center of the oven and preheat to 350°F. Heat the oil in a large ovenproof skillet over medium-high heat. Coat the chicken in flour, shaking off the excess. In batches, without crowding, add the chicken to the skillet and cook, turning once, until the chicken is nicely browned on both sides, about 6 minutes. Transfer the chicken to a platter, leaving the oil in the skillet.

2. Add the onion to the skillet and cook just until it begins to soften, about 3 minutes. Add the garlic, reduce the heat to low, and cook until the onion is translucent, about 3 minutes more. Stir in jalapeño, turmeric, and cumin and cook for a few seconds. Stir in the tomatoes with their juices, the broth, and lemon zest, and bring to a simmer. Return the chicken to the skillet.

3. Bake in the oven until the chicken shows no sign of pink when pierced in the thickest part, 20 to 30 minutes. If the tomato juices evaporate, add a few table-spoons of water. Serve hot.

roast chicken with ginger, garlic, and lemon

MAKES 4 SERVINGS

Few dishes say "home cooking" like a roast chicken. Sure, you can get rotisserie chicken at many markets or butcher shops, but there's a big sense of accomplishment when you bring your very own chicken to the table, burnished to a roasted golden brown. The relatively high oven temperature helps you achieve that gorgeous color. An under-the-skin paste of ginger, garlic, and lemon will perfume the flesh. Why not roast two chickens so you'll have leftovers for the next day?

One 3½-pound chicken

3 tablespoons extra-virgin olive oil

1 tablespoon minced fresh parsley

1 tablespoon peeled and minced fresh ginger

Grated zest of 1 lemon

½ teaspoon freshly ground black pepper

1. Position a rack in the center of the oven and preheat the oven to 400°F. Make a slit at the tip of the body cavity of the chicken to separate the skin from the flesh. Slip your fingertips underneath the skin and work your fingers around the breast and thigh areas to loosen the skin from the flesh.

2. Mix 2 tablespoons of the oil, the parsley, ginger, and lemon zest in a small bowl. Rub the parsley mixture under the loosened skin. Smooth and massage the skin to evenly distribute the parsley mixture. Place the chicken on a lightly oiled roasting rack (or fashion one out of a long strip of aluminum foil, twisted into a rope, and shaped into a ring) in a roasting pan. Brush the top of the chicken with the remaining 1 tablespoon of oil.

3. Roast until an instant-read thermometer inserted in the thickest part of the thigh, but not touching a bone, reads 170°F, about 1 hour.

4. Transfer the chicken to a platter and let stand for 10 to 15 minutes to redistribute the juices. Carve and serve hot.

not exactly italian sausages with peppers

MAKES 4 SERVINGS

The way most people make Italian sausage and peppers is to smother the sausage in lots of sautéed peppers. It's good, but I expand on the theme with plump, juicy tomatoes and a big handful of basil. And turkey sausage adds a healthy twist to this traditional dish. Try it spooned over pasta for a truly Italian experience.

2 tablespoons olive oil

1½ pounds Italian-style turkey sausages, cut on an angle into 2- to 3-inch lengths

2 medium red onions, cut into ¾-inch dice

2 large red bell peppers, cored, seeded, and cut into ¾-inch dice

6 garlic cloves, thinly sliced

7 ripe plum tomatoes, cut into ¾-inch dice

¼ cup coarsely chopped fresh basil

1 teaspoon dried oregano

Kosher salt and freshly ground black pepper to taste

1. Heat the oil in a large skillet over medium-high heat. Add the sausages and cook, stirring occasionally, until they are lightly browned, about 3 minutes.

2. Add the onions, bell peppers, and garlic. Cook, stirring often, until the vegetables soften, about 6 minutes. Add the tomatoes, basil, and oregano. Cook, stirring often, until the tomatoes and sausage are heated through, about 5 minutes more. Season with salt and pepper. Serve hot.

turkey and lamb cholent

MAKES 6 TO 8 SERVINGS

When Shabbat makes its weekly visit, cholent prepared in a slow cooker is the Saturday midday meal of choice for countless families. This filling dish has a reputation for being stodgy, but not my tasty version with bits of salami and jalapeño to provide a zesty kick to the familiar standby. While lamb is a popular ingredient in some cholent recipes, it is also expensive at kosher butcher shops, turning an Old Country casserole into a financial investment. But a single pound of lamb mixed with turkey thighs will yield meaty flavor without breaking the budget, making this truly a cholent to give thanks for.

2 tablespoons vegetable oil, or more as needed

2 large onions, chopped

3 carrots, chopped

1 jalapeño, thinly sliced into rounds (do not remove seeds)

6 garlic cloves, smashed under a knife and peeled

2 pounds turkey thighs, skin and bones removed, cut into 1½-inch chunks

1 pound boneless lamb stew meat, cut into 1½-inch chunks

¼ pound beef salami, cut into ½-inch chunks

4½ cups cold water, plus hot water as needed

One 6-ounce can tomato paste

1 pound baby new potatoes

1 pound "cholent mix" dried beans, or 1 cup each dried white kidney (cannellini), garbanzo (chickpeas), and kidney beans

¼ cup pearled barley

1½ tablespoons dried oregano

Two 3-inch cinnamon sticks

½ teaspoon freshly ground black pepper

Kosher salt to taste

1. Heat the oil in a large skillet over medium heat. Add the onions, carrots, jalapeño, and garlic. Cook, stirring occasionally, until the onion is softened, about 8 minutes. Transfer to the insert of a 5-quart slow cooker.

2. Add more vegetable oil to the skillet, if needed, and heat over medium-high heat. Add the turkey, lamb, and salami to the skillet and cook, stirring often, until they are lightly browned, about 8 minutes. Transfer the turkey and meat to the insert. Add 4½ cups water and the tomato paste to the skillet. Bring to a boil, scraping up the browned bits in the pan and dissolving the tomato paste. Pour into the insert. Add the potatoes, dried beans, barley, oregano, cinnamon sticks, and pepper and stir well. Add more hot water as needed to cover the beans by 1 inch.

3. Turn the slow cooker setting on high and cover. Cook until the cholent is visibly simmering, about 1 hour. If serving the next day, turn the setting to low and cook until ready to serve, 16 to 18 hours. If serving the same day, cook for 4 hours on high. Reduce the heat to low and continue cooking until the beans are tender, about 4 hours more.

4. Uncover and season with salt. Serve hot.

The Sabbath Slow Cooker

The slow cooker has become an essential tool for Sabbath cooking, as it allows Saturday's afternoon meal to cook without any intervention. It's a great piece of kitchen equipment, but there are drawbacks.

The steam created by the food in covered slow cookers has no place to go and will collect in the cooking insert. This liquid must be accounted for in the recipe, as it will also dilute the taste of the food. To defuse the situation, add another layer of flavor by sautéing vegetables to bring out their sweetness. Allow enough time to brown the meat and poultry, which will lightly caramelize the surface, adding more savory elements. Sure, you can dump everything in the pot and leave it at that, but frankly, the results are pretty boring, to say the least.

Here's one more very important trick to making slow-cooker cholent. As soon as all of the ingredients are in the cooking insert, turn the setting to high to allow them to come to a full boil. Then, adjust the setting to low for the rest of the cooking period. Without this initial start-up, the cholent could spoil—a sad occurrence that has been reported to me by some students. Eighteen hours is a long time for something to cook, but the heat from the full boil will discourage bacterial growth.

turkey osso bucco–style

MAKES 6 SERVINGS

Instead of veal shanks, which aren't easy to get kosher, substitute cubes of boneless turkey thighs to make this Italian-inspired dish. It is a simple chore to remove the skin and bones from turkey thighs for the stew. Serve this on top of spaghetti, and watch the kids gobble it up.

3 pounds turkey thighs

½ cup olive oil

½ cup all-purpose flour

2 medium onions, chopped

One 28-ounce can chopped tomatoes in juice, drained

1 cup dry white wine or additional chicken broth

6 garlic cloves, chopped

1½ tablespoons herbes de Provence (see page 91)

3 tablespoons chopped fresh rosemary

2 tablespoons chopped fresh oregano

1 quart chicken broth

6 medium carrots, chopped

4 medium celery ribs, chopped

Kosher salt and freshly ground black pepper to taste

1. Working with one thigh at a time, pull off and discard the skin. Using a sharp, thin knife, cut the meat from each side of the bone to get 2 large chunks. (You can save the bones and add them to the stew for extra flavor. If you do this, don't forget to remove them before serving!) Cut the meat into 1-inch cubes.

2. Heat ¼ cup of the oil in a Dutch oven over medium-high heat. In batches, coat the turkey cubes in flour, shaking off the excess flour, and add to the pot. Cook, turning the turkey occasionally, until browned on all sides, about 5 minutes. Using a slotted spoon, transfer the turkey to a plate.

3. Add the remaining ¼ cup of oil to the Dutch oven and heat. Add the onions and cook, stirring often, until they are translucent, about 5 minutes. Stir in the drained tomatoes, wine, garlic, herbes de Provence, rosemary, and oregano. Return the turkey to the pot, and add the broth, carrots, and celery. Bring to a boil over high heat.

4. Reduce the heat to medium and cover the pot. Simmer until the turkey is tender, about 45 minutes. Season with salt and pepper and serve hot.

Herbes de Provence

The hillsides in Provence are literally covered with rosemary, lavender, and thyme. These, and other herbs, find their way into this blend known as herbes de Provence. It used to be found only at specialty grocers, but with this recipe, you can make your own at home, with herbs you may already have in your spice cabinet.

Mix 1 tablespoon each dried basil, thyme, rosemary, and oregano, and 2 teaspoons fennel seed. If you have them, add 2 teaspoons each dried savory and culinary lavender (in other words, not preserved lavender for potpourri). Store in a covered container in a cool dark place for up to 6 months. Makes about ⅓ cup.

herbed turkey patties on braised escarole

MAKES 4 SERVINGS

Kids love burgers (well, who doesn't really?). These pan-fried patties, made with ground turkey instead of the familiar ground beef, are lighter, but more flavorful than typical burgers. The crisp coating is a counterpoint for the tender escarole.

1 medium onion, finely chopped

2 garlic cloves, minced

2 tablespoons vegetable oil, such as canola, plus more for frying

2 tablespoons chopped fresh parsley

2 teaspoons chopped fresh thyme or ½ teaspoon dried thyme

2 teaspoons chopped fresh rosemary or ½ teaspoon dried rosemary

2 large eggs, beaten

½ cup plus 2 tablespoons plain dried bread crumbs

½ teaspoon kosher salt

½ teaspoon freshly ground black pepper

2 pounds ground turkey

Escarole (see page 198; omit Toasted Bread Crumbs)

1. Combine the onion, garlic, and oil in a medium skillet over medium heat. (Starting the vegetables in a cold skillet will keep them from browning.) Cook, stirring occasionally, until the onion is translucent, about 6 minutes. Remove from the heat and stir in the parsley, thyme, and rosemary. Scrape into a large bowl and cool for at least 30 minutes. Add the eggs, 2 tablespoons bread crumbs, salt, pepper, and the turkey meat to the bowl and mix just until combined. Shape into 16 small patties.

2. Pour enough oil into a very large skillet to come ¼ inch up the sides of the skillet. Heat the oil over medium-high heat until it is very hot but not smoking. Spread the remaining ½ cup bread crumbs on a plate. Dip each patty on both sides into the bread crumbs, shake off the excess crumbs, and place in the skillet. Reduce the heat to medium and cook until the underside is golden brown, about 3 minutes. Adjust the heat as needed so that the patties cook steadily but don't burn—they need to cook through. Turn the patties and cook until the other side is golden, about 3 minutes more. Transfer the patties to paper towels to drain briefly and prepare the escarole.

3. To serve, use a slotted spoon to heap the escarole onto each of 4 dinner plates. Top each with 4 patties. Serve hot.

Fresh Herbs

One of the biggest revelations I had in culinary school concerned fresh herbs. The bright flavors hit me over the head like a cartoon character with a baseball bat. What had I been missing all my life? So my family and I can have fresh herbs without running to the store, we have an herb garden that grows full tilt all summer long. We just snip off whatever we need for the day's cooking. Here are a few tips for working with fresh herbs, whether you grow them yourself or buy them.

Never try to chop wet herbs. After rinsing (I swish the entire bunch in a bowl of cold water) and shaking off the excess water, stand them up in a small glass and refrigerate them overnight to evaporate any surface moisture. If you want to chop the herbs right away, spin them in a salad spinner or pat completely dry with paper towels.

To use extra or leftover herbs, chop them and incorporate into one of the compound butters listed on page 129, or purée the herbs in a mini blender with a small amount of extra-virgin olive oil to make an herb pesto. Scrape the pesto into a small container, film the top with a little more oil, cover, and refrigerate for up to 3 weeks. When a recipe would benefit from a bit of fresh herb flavor, stir a spoonful of the pesto into the dish.

meat

I've said it many times: What kosher meat may lack in tenderness, it more than makes up for in flavor. In traditional kosher cooking, cuts like flanken, brisket, and stew meat are braised, a process that melts the tough parts into submission. There's nothing like a long-simmered stew, but they are sometimes difficult to fit into the typical work-week schedule. We now make them on our days off, and serve them a day or so later. As a bonus (as if having tender brisket in the refrigerator isn't reward enough), these dishes are even tastier when refrigerated overnight before serving, because the flavors really get a chance to mingle. And don't forget that these dishes freeze well, too. How great is it to come home, thinking that there's nothing in the house to eat, to find truly homemade beef stew, ready to go?

For red-meat family suppers on crazy-busy weeknights, we turn to steaks, chops, and ground meat. When cooking kosher meat, keep in mind that it has already been salted. To remove some of the saltiness, it helps to do a little preliminary work. Skirt steak, a thin cut that absorbs quite a bit of salt, should be soaked in cold water for at least 30 minutes. When adding cooked ground beef to casseroles, pasta sauce, and the like, add the beef to a pot of boiling water and cook for a few minutes to remove excess fat, as well as salt. These two little tricks will improve your red-meat dishes enormously.

When gathering the recipes for this chapter, I noticed how often Ali and I make recipes that were inspired by our mothers' cooking, such as meat loaf, franks and beans, and kielbasa with sauerkraut. These retro-style dishes, with a few updates in seasoning, are still crowd-pleasers. Cooking handed-down recipes is a pleasure that connects our children with their grandparents.

grilled skirt steak with mint chimichurri

MAKES 6 TO 8 SERVINGS

In Argentina, they serve a pungent, herb-based sauce called chimichurri with their grilled steaks. I've fooled around with the ingredients to come up with a mint variation that does double duty as a marinade and serving sauce for skirt steaks.

Mint Chimichurri

1½ cups packed fresh mint leaves

½ cup packed fresh parsley leaves

5 garlic cloves, chopped

1 jalapeño, seeds and ribs removed, quartered lengthwise

1 teaspoon dried oregano

4 bay leaves

1 teaspoon kosher salt

½ teaspoon freshly ground black pepper

½ cup distilled white vinegar

½ cup extra-virgin olive oil

3 pounds skirt steak, soaked in water for 30 minutes, drained,
    and cut crosswise into 4 pieces

1. To make the chimichurri: Combine the mint, parsley, garlic, jalapeño, oregano, bay leaves, salt, and pepper in a food processor or blender, and pulse until coarsely chopped. With the machine running, add the vinegar, oil, and ½ cup water, and process, occasionally stopping the machine to scrape down the sides of the container, until the mixture is smooth. Pour 1 cup of the chimichurri into a serving bowl, cover, and refrigerate until ready to use as a sauce.

2. Pour the remaining chimichurri into a large glass or ceramic baking dish. Add the skirt steaks and turn to coat them on all sides. Cover and refrigerate, preferably at least 2 and up to 4 hours (but even a short marinade while the grill heats up is fine).

3. Build a charcoal fire in an outdoor grill and let burn until the coals are covered with white ashes. (For a gas grill, preheat on high.) Lightly oil the grill grate. Remove the steaks from the marinade, discarding the marinade. Grill, turning once, until the steaks are lightly browned and feel soft with a little resistance when pressed in the center, about 7 minutes for medium-rare meat, or longer if desired.

4. Transfer the steaks to a carving board and let stand 5 minutes. Cut the steaks crosswise with the grain (not across the grain, as for brisket) into thin slices. Serve with the bowl of chimichurri passed on the side.

grilled skirt steak
with roasted vegetable salsa

Here's another recipe for a backyard grill-out (although you could also pan-fry the skirt steak on the stove in a heavy skillet). Skirt steak is a powerhouse of beef flavor—just be sure to cut it into thin slices *with* the grain for the best texture. I always soak thin cuts of beef, such as skirt steak, to remove some of the excess salt that is absorbed during kashering—thicker cuts don't need soaking. The salsa should be bright and almost crunchy, not soft—a light roasting brings out the flavor, but shouldn't change the texture too much.

Chipotle Salsa

2 bunches scallions, ends trimmed (about 16 scallions)

4 ripe plum tomatoes, cut lengthwise in half

2 large red bell peppers, cored, seeded, and cut lengthwise into six wedges

1 medium red onion, cut lengthwise into six wedges

2 jalapeños, cut lengthwise in half (do not remove seeds unless you want
    a very mild salsa)

¼ cup extra-virgin olive oil

Kosher salt and freshly ground black pepper to taste

1½ tablespoons fresh lime juice

1 tablespoon chopped fresh cilantro

½ teaspoon ground chipotle chile (see Note)

⅛ teaspoon cayenne pepper, optional

2 pounds skirt steak

1. To make the salsa, position a rack in the center of the oven and preheat the oven to 450°F. Lightly oil a large baking sheet.

2. Arrange the scallions, tomatoes, bell peppers, onion, and jalapeños in separate areas on the baking sheet. The vegetables may be crowded, but don't worry; the steam they create will help them cook more quickly and evenly. Keeping the vegetables separate, drizzle with the oil and mix to coat them. Season with the salt and pepper. Roast until the scallions wilt and the tomatoes begin to soften, about 10 minutes. Using tongs, transfer the scallions and tomatoes to a chopping board. Continue roasting the peppers, onion, and jalapeños until they are slightly softened, about 10 minutes more, and transfer them to the chopping board.

3. Chop the vegetables with a large knife into ½-inch dice and place in a bowl. Add the lime juice, cilantro, chipotle, and cayenne, if using. Season again with salt and pepper. Set aside until ready to serve.

4. Meanwhile, soak the skirt steak in cold water to cover for 30 minutes to remove excess salt. Pat dry with paper towels.

5. Build a charcoal fire in an outdoor grill and let it burn until the coals are covered with white ash. Or preheat a gas grill to high. Lightly oil the grill grate.

6. Grill the steaks, turning once, until medium-rare, about 3½ minutes per side, or longer, if desired. Let stand for a few minutes. Hold the knife at a slight diagonal and thinly slice each steak crosswise along its length, with the grain. Serve the sliced steak topped with a large spoonful of salsa.

NOTE Pure ground chiles, such as the sweet, hot ancho and the smoky, fiery chipotle, can be found at Latino grocers and in the spice aisle at many supermarkets. Kosher chiles are available by mail order from www.chefjeffgourmet.com, 1-888-562-4331. Chili powder, which is usually a relatively mild New Mexican chile combined with seasonings like oregano, cumin, and garlic powder, can be substituted, but the flavor of the pure ground chile is more distinct.

the nathan family meat loaves

MAKES 2 MEAT LOAVES, 4 TO 6 SERVINGS EACH

Sometimes it takes the same amount of time to make a lot of food as it does a smaller amount of food. For example, when we make meat loaf at home, we always make two loaves and almost a quart of gravy because it takes literally no extra effort. Meat Loaf Number Two is slated for the freezer, but usually it doesn't last long enough to reach that state, having been devoured as the main course of another meal or tucked into sandwiches. Like every family, we have our own special recipe that we believe would kick the *tuchas* of any rival, and here it is.

1 cup dried plain bread crumbs

¼ cup chopped fresh parsley

1 large egg plus 3 large egg yolks

3 tablespoons onion powder

6 garlic cloves, finely chopped, plus 3 garlic cloves, cut in half crosswise

1 tablespoon dried oregano

1 teaspoon dried basil

1 teaspoon freshly ground black pepper, plus more for gravy

3 pounds ground beef

1 medium onion, thickly sliced

¼ cup all-purpose flour

1 quart chicken broth

Kosher salt and freshly ground black pepper to taste

1. Position a rack in the center of the oven and preheat the oven to 350°F. Lightly oil a flameproof roasting pan.

2. To make the meat loaves, mix the bread crumbs, ½ cup water, parsley, egg and yolks, onion powder, chopped garlic, oregano, basil, and pepper in a large bowl. Add the beef, and use your hands to quickly mix everything together just until barely combined. Do not overmix, or the meat loaf will be heavy.

3. Scatter the sliced onion and garlic halves in the bottom of the roasting pan to flavor the gravy. Form the meat mixture into two loaves, each about 8 inches long and 3 inches wide, and place on top of the onions and garlic. Bake, uncovered, until the meat loaves *show no sign of pink* when prodded in the center with the tip of a knife (about 165°F on a meat thermometer), about 45 minutes.

4. Transfer the meat loaves to a serving platter. Place the roasting pan with the onions, garlic, and pan drippings over 2 burners on medium-high heat. Sprinkle the flour into the pan and whisk to make a paste that is chunky with the onions and garlic. Whisk in the broth and bring to a boil, whisking occasionally. Reduce the heat to medium-low and simmer until the gravy thickens, about 5 minutes. Season the gravy with salt and pepper. Strain the gravy into a bowl, or serve it with the onions and garlic intact.

5. Slice the meat loaf and serve hot, with the gravy passed on the side.

barbecue chili

MAKES 6 TO 8 SERVINGS

Chili is one of those dishes that I keep playing with, even though every time I make it, I feel that it's perfect and I'll never use another recipe. I even won a chili contest once, so you'd think I'd rest easy. And yet here's another one, this time flavored with sweet-and-spicy barbecue sauce (use your favorite store-bought brand). The first step removes the excess fat and improves the flavor of kosher ground beef, which tends to be quite fatty. Keep this tip in mind whenever you want to add ground beef to a soup, stew, or pasta sauce. For a milder chili that the tenderfeet in the family will enjoy, use the chili powder option, not the chipotle powder, and remove the seeds and ribs from the jalapeños before chopping.

2 pounds ground beef

3 tablespoons canola oil

1 large onion, chopped

2 jalapeños, chopped, including seeds and ribs

3 garlic cloves, chopped

2 tablespoons onion powder

2 tablespoons garlic powder

2 tablespoons ground chipotle chile or additional chili powder

1 tablespoon chili powder

One 28-ounce can crushed tomatoes in purée

One 15- to 19-ounce can red kidney beans, drained and rinsed

One 15- to 19-ounce can black beans, drained and rinsed

2 cups store-bought barbecue sauce

1 tablespoon liquid smoke

Kosher salt and freshly ground black pepper to taste

1. Place the ground beef in a large, deep skillet and add enough cold water to cover. Bring to a boil over medium-high heat. Reduce the heat to medium to keep the liquid at a brisk simmer. Cook, breaking up the meat with a spoon, until it is in pea-size pieces and turns gray, about 5 minutes. Drain in a colander (it will not smell wonderful), letting the water and fat drain away. Set the beef aside.

2. Heat the oil in a Dutch oven over medium heat. Add the onion and cook until translucent, about 5 minutes. Stir in the jalapeños, garlic, onion and garlic powders, ground chipotle, and chili powder. Add the reserved beef, crushed tomatoes, kidney and black beans and bring to a simmer, stirring often. Reduce the heat to low and simmer for 10 minutes. Stir in the barbecue sauce and simmer to blend the flavors, about 10 minutes. Stir in the liquid smoke and season with the salt and pepper just before serving. Serve hot, ladled into bowls.

Spice It Up

People are often surprised to see onion powder and garlic powder in my recipes. Now don't get me wrong—I would never tell you to use them by themselves as a substitute for the real things. But when I want an extra kick of savory flavor, especially in ground beef dishes such as this chili, I use them without shame. They really do the trick.

blackened burgers
with avocado mayonnaise

MAKES 4 SERVINGS

Nothing hits the spot like a good old burger. This is the way we like them at our house, coated in spices and grilled, with a creamy avocado mayonnaise. We usually offer the whole gamut of condiments—tomato, lettuce, onions, and pickles. But if you are in the mood for a really hot culinary experience, serve the burgers with salsa instead of the traditional go-withs.

Avocado Mayonnaise

1 ripe avocado, pitted and peeled

2 tablespoons fresh lemon juice

½ cup mayonnaise

2 tablespoons chopped fresh cilantro

Kosher salt and freshly ground black pepper to taste

2 pounds ground beef

⅓ cup Blackened Spice Blend (page 139)

4 hamburger buns, split

Tomato slices, lettuce leaves, onion rings, and pickle slices, for serving

1. To make the mayonnaise, mash the avocado and lemon juice together in a small bowl. Stir in the mayonnaise and cilantro, and season with salt and pepper. Cover and let stand while making the burgers.

2. Build a charcoal fire in an outdoor grill and let it burn until the coals are covered with white ash. Do not spread the coals out, but leave them in a heap in the center of the grill. (For a gas grill, preheat on high. Leave one burner on high and turn the other burner or burners off.)

3. Handling the ground beef gently, form it into 4 patties about 4 inches across. Spread the spice mixture on a plate. Dip both sides of each burger into the spices.

4. Place the burgers on the grill, directly over the coals (or over the high burner), and cover. Grill until the underside is browned, about 1½ minutes. Turn the burgers, cover again, and brown the other side, about 1½ minutes more. Move the burgers to an area not directly over the coals (or to the off burner). Cover and continue grilling the burgers until they are medium-rare, about 4 minute more. Transfer the burgers to a platter.

5. Toast the buns on the grill. Serve the burgers with avocado mayonnaise, along with the buns, tomatoes, lettuce, onions, and pickles on the side.

brisket with port wine and mushroom sauce

MAKES 8 TO 10 SERVINGS

Tender, melt-in-your-mouth brisket is one of my favorite dishes to serve to friends and family. Every time I make it at home, I do it a little differently than the way before. My latest version simmers the meat in rich port wine with lots of mushrooms, so much the better for a deep, dark sauce that is made for pouring over noodles. It's a waste of time to only make a single three-pound brisket, so this recipe makes enough for precious leftovers. If you have the time, make the brisket the day ahead, which makes it easier to slice thinly.

3 tablespoons canola oil

Two 3-pound first-cut beef briskets, trimmed

2 medium onions, halved lengthwise and thinly sliced into half-moons

8 garlic cloves, halved

1¾ cups tawny or ruby port

2 pounds assorted fresh mushrooms (see page 35), sliced or quartered, depending on size

3 bay leaves

⅓ cup all-purpose flour

Kosher salt and freshly ground black pepper to taste

1. Position a rack in the center of the oven and preheat to 325°F.

2. Heat the oil in a very large, deep Dutch oven over medium-high heat. One at a time, add the briskets and cook, turning once, until browned on both sides, about 10 minutes. Transfer the brisket to a platter.

3. Add the onions and garlic to the pot and cook, stirring occasionally, until the onions are lightly browned, about 10 minutes. Add the port, mushrooms, and bay leaves and bring to a simmer, scraping up any browned bits in the pot with a wooden spoon. Simmer for 5 minutes. Return the briskets and any juices on the platter to the pot. Add enough cold water to barely cover the briskets and bring to a simmer over high heat. Cover tightly. Place in the oven and bake until the briskets are fork-tender, about 2 hours and 15 minutes. Remove the bay leaves.

4. Uncover and let the briskets cool in the pot. Cover and refrigerate until the next day.

5. Scrape off and discard any hardened fat on the surface of the cooking liquid. Transfer the briskets to a carving board and slice thinly across the grain.

6. Meanwhile, bring the cooking liquid to a boil over high heat. Taste, and if the flavor needs concentrating, boil for a few minutes to evaporate excess liquid.

7. Whisk the flour and water together in a medium bowl to dissolve the flour. Whisk in about 2 cups of the cooking liquid. Whisk this liquid into the pot. Reduce the heat to medium-low and simmer until the sauce thickens and has no raw flour taste, about 5 minutes. Season with salt and pepper. Return the sliced briskets to the sauce, and simmer until heated through, 5 to 10 minutes. Serve hot with the sauce.

korean-style short ribs

MAKES 6 TO 8 SERVINGS

Korean cuisine has a grilling tradition every bit as entrenched as our American barbecue. Their rich marinade is always on the sweet side, packed with scallions and garlic.
And flanken happens to be one of the most popular cuts for grilling Korean-style. Note
that the flanken is not long cooked to tenderness here, and will be somewhat chewy.
Serve it with my version of the Korean pickle, kim chee, and lots of rice.

2 cups soy sauce

8 scallions, white and green parts, coarsely chopped

1 cup packed light brown sugar

1 cup mirin (see Note, page 135) or sweet white wine, such as Riesling

½ cup rice wine vinegar

½ cup dark Asian sesame oil

½ cup minced garlic (the store-bought variety in the jar is fine)

¼ cup minced fresh ginger

2 teaspoons freshly ground black pepper

6 pounds beef flanken (cross-cut beef ribs)

My Kim Chee (page 200), for serving

Hot cooked rice, for serving

1. Mix the soy sauce, scallions, brown sugar, mirin, vinegar, sesame oil, garlic, ginger, and black pepper in a large bowl. Divide the beef among two zippered plastic
bags. Add equal amounts of the marinade and close the bags. Refrigerate for at
least 8 hours and up to 12 hours.

2. Build a charcoal fire in an outdoor grill and let burn until the coals are covered
with white ash. (For a gas grill, preheat on high.) Lightly oil the grill grate.

3. Remove the beef from the marinade. Grill, turning occasionally, until the meat
is well browned and medium-rare, about 8 minutes, or longer, if you prefer.

4. For each serving, place 2 or 3 lengths of flanken on a plate, top with kim chee
and a mound of rice. Serve hot.

provençal beef stew

MAKES 4 TO 6 SERVINGS

Any stew that sports the Provençal name will be deeply aromatic, and this one lives up to its reputation. The stew is cooked at higher temperatures than usual to save time. The beef and vegetables provide such flavor that I don't use stock as a liquid, but you can do so if you wish.

4 tablespoons olive oil

2 pounds beef stew, such as chuck, cut into 1-inch cubes

½ teaspoon freshly ground black pepper

1 large onion, chopped

3 garlic cloves, finely chopped

3 tablespoon all-purpose flour

4 cups cold water

½ cup hearty red wine, such as Cabernet Sauvignon

4 teaspoons herbes de Provence (see page 91)

2 medium baking potatoes, such as Burbank or russet, peeled and cut into ¾-inch dice

1 large carrot, cut into ¾-inch dice

1 large parsnip, cut into ¾-inch dice

Kosher salt to taste

1. Heat the oil in a Dutch oven over medium-high heat. Season the beef with pepper. In batches, without crowding, add the beef and cook, turning occasionally, until browned, about 5 minutes. Return all the beef to the pot. Add the onion and garlic and cook, stirring often, until the onion softens, about 5 minutes. Sprinkle with the flour and stir well. Stir in the cold water, wine, and herbes de Provence, and bring to a boil over high heat. Reduce the heat to medium and cook at a brisk simmer for 20 minutes.

2. Meanwhile, preheat the oven to 350°F. Sir in the potatoes, carrot, and parsnip and cover again. Place in the oven and bake until the meat is tender, about 30 minutes more.

3. Skim off the fat, then season with salt and pepper to taste, keeping in mind that the stew meat will have been salted by the butcher. Serve hot.

lamb chops with eggplant aioli

MAKES 4 SERVINGS

Roasted eggplant is mixed with roasted garlic and mayonnaise to make a thick sauce to complement the broiled lamb chops. In Provence, this garlic mayonnaise is called aioli (eye-OH-lee), but you can call it garlic mayonnaise unless you're practicing your French. If you feel like tossing the chops onto the outdoor grill, go ahead. This recipe will please the grown-ups who like high-flavor dishes, as well as kids who like their food plain, as the aioli is served on the side.

Eggplant Aioli

1 large eggplant, about 1⅓ pounds

4 roasted garlic cloves (see page 203), or use store-bought roasted garlic

2 tablespoons fresh lemon juice

⅓ cup mayonnaise

¼ cup extra-virgin olive oil

Kosher salt and freshly ground black pepper to taste

Lamb Chops

8 shoulder lamb chops, about 7 ounces each

½ teaspoon freshly ground black pepper

¼ cup extra-virgin olive oil

1 tablespoon herbes de Provence (see page 91)

1. To make the aioli, position a rack in the center of the oven and preheat the oven to 350°F. Line a baking sheet with aluminum foil (for easy cleanup). Pierce the eggplant a couple of times with a fork. Place on the baking sheet and bake until the eggplant is tender (it will collapse), about 1 hour. Cool until easy to handle. Scrape the soft flesh from the eggplant, and discard the peel.

2. Pulse the eggplant, roasted garlic, and lemon juice in a food processor until the vegetables are coarsely chopped. Stop the machine and add the mayonnaise. With the machine running, slowly add the oil through the feed tube. Season with salt and pepper. Transfer to a serving bowl, cover, and set aside.

3. For the lamb chops, position a broiler rack 6 inches from the source of heat and preheat the broiler. Sprinkle the lamb chops on both sides with the pepper. Toss the lamb chops in a large bowl with the oil. Sprinkle the lamb on both sides with the herbs and rub the herbs into the lamb.

4. Broil the lamb chops, turning once, until lightly browned on both sides, about 8 minutes for medium-rare, or longer, if desired. Serve immediately, with the eggplant aioli passed on the side.

rosemary lamb rib chops with roasted root vegetables

MAKES 4 SERVINGS

The combination of rosemary and lamb is pretty hard to beat. I've grilled the rib lamb chops in this recipe because I think a little charcoal flavor goes a long way, but of course, they can be broiled, if you wish. If you don't have a separate broiler and need to use the oven to cook the chops, cover the roasted vegetables with aluminum foil— they'll stay hot for the ten minutes it takes to broil the chops.

Roasted Root Vegetables

4 large carrots, cut into sticks about 2 inches long and ¼ inch wide

4 large parsnips, cut into sticks about 2 inches long and ¼ inch wide

¼ cup extra-virgin olive oil

2 tablespoons coarsely chopped fresh rosemary

3 tablespoons water

Kosher salt and freshly ground black pepper to taste

Rosemary Lamb Chops

½ cup extra-virgin olive oil

½ cup coarsely chopped fresh rosemary

16 lamb rib chops, cut about ¾ inch thick

Freshly ground black pepper to taste

1. To roast the vegetables, position a rack in the center of the oven and preheat the oven to 450°F. Line a large rimmed baking sheet with aluminum foil.

2. Combine the carrots, parsnips, oil, rosemary, and water (don't forget the water, or the vegetables may scorch) in a large bowl and toss well. Season with salt and pepper. Spread on the baking sheet. Roast until the vegetables are tender and lightly browned, about 25 minutes. To keep the vegetables hot, turn off the oven and prop the oven door barely open with the handle of a wooden spoon. They are also great warm or cooled to room temperature.

3. Meanwhile, for the lamb chops, build a charcoal fire in an outdoor grill and let burn until the coals are covered with white ash. For a gas grill, preheat on high. Lightly oil the grill grate.

4. Combine the oil and rosemary in a large bowl. Add the lamb chops and toss to coat with the rosemary oil. Season the chops with pepper. Place on the grill and cover. Grill, turning occasionally, until medium-rare, about 10 minutes.

5. Place the vegetables in the center of a large platter, and arrange the lamb chops on top. Serve hot.

The Family Cookbook

I often hear people exclaim how they never got the recipe for Grandma's potato kugel or Aunt Sarah's rugelach before they passed away. One way to solve the problem is a family cookbook.

Holiday meals are a great place to start, as they are often potlucks where friends and family bring their specialties to the table. Ask each guest to provide a written recipe of their contribution, and have someone on hand to take a photograph of the dish (while it is still fresh and looks its best).

You have two options for archiving: the old-fashioned scrapbook method or the digital approach. For an actual scrapbook, keep collecting the recipes until you have enough to make a book; a three-ring binder works well. The recipes and photographs can be photocopied, with the originals separately stored in a safe place. Photocopying also makes the cookbook easy to reproduce and send to other relatives.

If you prefer a digital archive, scan the recipes and photos and keep them in a "cookbook file" on your home computer. The recipes could also be typed out, but I like seeing the person's handwriting and approach to recipe writing. (Were they an "A" personality that wrote out "2 tablespoons sugar," or did they use the more casual "2 TB"?) Sharing the recipes is merely a matter of clicking a few keys.

There is always the problem of the relative who doesn't measure as they cook, and uses "a pinch of this and a handful of that." The only solution is to get in the kitchen with the person, and supply your own measuring utensils to keep track of the action. It's a bit more effort, but I guarantee that it will make for a fun, memorable time spent with a loved one.

"franks" and beans casserole

MAKES 4 TO 6 SERVINGS

In our family, we call this "Franks" and Beans Casserole even though we usually use knockwurst. This is because my mom used to make something like this rib-sticking one-dish meal with frankfurters. The pastrami is optional, but it does add another layer of peppery, meaty flavor to the beans. So toss a green salad to serve on the side and get ready for an old-fashioned family supper.

3 tablespoons canola oil, plus more as needed

1 pound knockwurst, cut on a slight diagonal into ½-inch-thick slices

3 large onions, chopped

½ pound pastrami, cut into ½-inch cubes, optional

Two 28-ounce cans vegetarian baked beans

⅓ cup pure maple syrup or maple-flavored pancake syrup

¼ cup spicy brown mustard

¼ cup ketchup

1 tablespoon liquid smoke

Freshly ground black pepper to taste

1. Position a rack in the center of the oven and preheat to 400°F.

2. Heat the oil in a large skillet over medium-high heat. Add the knockwurst slices and cook, turning occasionally, until lightly browned. Transfer the slices to a plate, leaving the drippings in the pan.

3. Add more oil to the skillet, if needed. Add the onions and reduce the heat to medium. Cook, stirring often, until golden, about 15 minutes. If using the pastrami, move the onions to one side of the skillet. Add the pastrami to the empty side of the skillet and cook until the pastrami begins to crisp, 3 to 5 minutes. Add ½ cup water to the skillet and stir with a wooden spoon to scrape up all the browned bits in the pan. Stir in the beans, maple syrup, mustard, ketchup, and liquid smoke. Stir in the reserved knockwurst.

4. Transfer to a 3-quart ovenproof casserole. Bake, uncovered, until the beans are bubbling and the top is glazed, about 30 minutes. Let stand for a few minutes, then serve hot, with a green salad.

kielbasa with spiced sauerkraut and apples

MAKES 6 TO 8 SERVINGS

At first glance, this looks like something your nana might make, if she came from Eastern Europe, but there are a lot of little tricks that make this dish special. Brown sugar, apple juice, and cider vinegar help sweeten the sauerkraut, and a trio of spices makes it a heck of a lot more interesting than Nana's. Like many dishes from the Old Country, it tastes much better than it looks. I know that doesn't sound too encouraging, but a side dish of small red-skinned potatoes, boiled in their jackets and sprinkled with olive oil and chopped fresh parsley, would brighten things up.

3 tablespoons extra-virgin olive oil

1 large onion, halved lengthwise and thinly sliced into half-moons

3 garlic cloves, chopped

1/2 cup packed light brown sugar

1 1/2 teaspoons caraway seeds

1 teaspoon ground cumin

1 teaspoon ground allspice

2 pounds kielbasa, cut on a slight diagonal into 3-inch lengths

2 pounds refrigerated sauerkraut, drained and rinsed

One 28-ounce can crushed tomatoes

3 Golden Delicious or Granny Smith apples, peeled, cored, and cut into thick wedges

1/2 cup apple juice

2 tablespoons cider vinegar

Kosher salt and freshly ground black pepper to taste

1. Heat the oil in a large saucepan over medium heat. Add the onion and garlic and cook, stirring occasionally, until the onion is translucent, about 8 minutes. Stir in the brown sugar, caraway seeds, cumin, and allspice. Cook, stirring often, until the spices are fragrant, about 1 minute. Add the kielbasa and cook for 5 minutes.

2. Stir in the sauerkraut, tomatoes, apples, apple juice, and vinegar and bring to a simmer. Reduce the heat to medium-low. Partially cover the pan and simmer until the kielbasa is heated through, about 25 minutes. Season with salt and pepper. Serve hot.

fish

Lush salmon, mild sea bass, meaty tuna—they all have distinct flavors and require slightly different cooking approaches. But there's one thing that they have in common: They are great for quick family suppers.

Overcooking is fish's enemy, so it rarely takes more than a half-hour to cook most seafood recipes. And the choice of cooking possibilities is practically endless. When we want a celebratory meal (excellent report cards are a good excuse), we'll serve the Tarragon Salmon Fillets with Vegetable Ragout on page 118. For a fun-to-eat main course with a crunchy coating, Crispy Sole with Parsley and Chives (page 125) is hard to beat. If the weather is blustery and we need something warm, we'll simmer up a pot of Salmon and Fennel Stew (page 120). We are never without a selection of compound butters in the freezer (see page 129), so one of our favorite fast suppers is to grill or sauté the fish of the day topped with a pat of flavored butter. Roasted, baked, sautéed, braised, grilled, fried—it is not such a mystery choosing which fish to prepare, but how to prepare it.

Rich in protein, vitamins, and minerals, fish is much lower in fat than red meat or poultry. Even the so-called fatty fish, such as salmon and tuna, are loaded with the omega-3 fatty acids that can lower blood cholesterol levels—one reason to make fish a mainstay of the family supper table.

Perhaps the biggest challenge when preparing fish is finding a reliable market for your purchases. More than any other food, fish is very perishable. So when you find a market that you like, let them know that you appreciate their quality.

tarragon salmon fillets with vegetable ragout

MAKES 4 SERVINGS

Salmon and a colorful collection of vegetables, brought together with tarragon and lemon, make an elegant dish that started out on my restaurant menu. The kids liked it so much that I now make this simplified version at home. Grill the salmon outdoors if you wish, or pan-grill it in a ridged pan.

Vegetable Ragout

1 tablespoon unsalted butter

1 tablespoon olive oil

4 garlic cloves, minced

$\frac{1}{8}$ teaspoon ground fennel seed, optional (see page 39)

5 ounces shiitake mushrooms, stems discarded, caps sliced

4 ounces sugar snap peas, trimmed

$\frac{1}{2}$ pint grape tomatoes or halved cherry tomatoes

$\frac{3}{4}$ cup Vegetable Broth (page 44) or vegetable bouillon

3 tablespoons fresh lemon juice

1 teaspoon chopped fresh tarragon

Four 7- to 8-ounce salmon fillets, skinned

2 tablespoons extra-virgin olive oil

2 tablespoons chopped fresh tarragon

Kosher salt and freshly ground black pepper to taste

2 tablespoons unsalted butter, cut into bits, chilled

1. Position a broiler rack 6 inches from the source of heat and preheat the broiler.

2. To make the ragout, melt the butter with the oil in a large skillet over medium heat. Add the garlic and fennel and cook, stirring often, until the garlic gives off its aroma, about 1 minute. Add the shiitakes and cook, stirring occasionally, for about 4 minutes. Stir in the sugar snap peas and cook for 1 minute. Add the tomatoes, broth, lemon juice, and tarragon. Bring to a simmer. Cook, stirring often, until the tomatoes are heated through, about 3 minutes. Remove from the heat, partially cover with a lid, and keep warm.

3. Meanwhile, brush the salmon fillets on both sides with the oil, sprinkle with the tarragon, and season with salt and pepper. Oil the broiler rack. Broil the fish, skinned side down, 8 to 10 minutes or until the fish is opaque in the center with a tinge of rose color when prodded with the tip of a sharp knife. Place each salmon fillet on a dinner plate.

4. Add the chilled butter to the vegetables. Stir with a wooden spoon, being careful not to break up the vegetables, until the butter melts. Season the ragout with salt and pepper. Spoon the ragout over each fillet and serve immediately.

salmon and fennel stew

MAKES 6 TO 8 SERVINGS

Stews are a simple way to serve a hungry family, and this one's no exception—put out some crusty bread, add a salad, and you're golden. Few vegetables complement fish like fennel (sometimes incorrectly called anise). In this wonderfully fragrant stew, other ingredients play along to give it an indescribably irresistible aroma. Hopefully, your fennel bulb will come with the fronds still attached to chop and use as a flavorful and colorful garnish—not that the stew isn't good-looking without it.

2 tablespoons brandy or additional fish stock

¼ teaspoon crumbled saffron threads

1½ cups Israeli couscous (about 8 ounces)

3 tablespoons extra-virgin olive oil

1 medium onion, chopped

1 celery rib, finely chopped

½ cup finely chopped fennel bulb

8 garlic cloves, finely chopped

½ jalapeño, seeded and finely chopped

½ cup dry white wine

Grated zest of 1 orange

1½ cups Fish Stock (page 43) or Vegetable Broth (page 44)

1 cup crushed tomatoes

2 pounds salmon fillets, skinned and cut into 1-inch pieces

¼ pound smoked salmon, cut into ⅛-inch dice

1 tablespoon chopped fresh basil

½ teaspoon chopped fresh thyme or ¼ teaspoon dried thyme

½ teaspoon ground chipotle chile or ¼ teaspoon cayenne pepper

Kosher salt and freshly ground black pepper to taste

Chopped fennel fronds, for garnish, optional

1. Mix the brandy and saffron in a small bowl, and let steep for 15 minutes and up to 1 hour. For the couscous, bring a medium saucepan of lightly salted water to a boil over high heat. Add the couscous and cook until tender, about 10 minutes. Drain, rinse under cold water, and set aside.

2. Meanwhile, heat the oil in a very large, deep skillet over medium heat. Add the onion, celery, fennel, garlic, and jalapeño. Cook, stirring often, until the vegetables soften, about 5 minutes. Add the brandy mixture, wine, and orange zest and cook until the wine is reduced by about half, 2 to 3 minutes. Add the stock and tomatoes and bring to a simmer. Cover and cook to blend the flavors, 10 to 12 minutes.

3. Add the salmon to the skillet and stir. Cook until the salmon turns opaque, 3 to 5 minutes. Stir in the reserved couscous, smoked salmon, basil, thyme, and chipotle powder and heat through. Season with salt and pepper.

4. Ladle the stew into bowls and sprinkle each serving with the chopped fennel fronds, if using. Serve hot.

roasted salmon fillets with herbed white beans

MAKES 4 SERVINGS

I've served many different kinds of fish with cannellini, but the meaty quality of salmon seems to be the best foil for the creaminess of these beans. Other so-called oily fish, such as grilled tuna or sautéed whiting, also work well. If you've previously only grilled or broiled salmon, get ready to learn a new trick, because roasting is another quick, salmon-friendly cooking method: Once the oven is preheated, dinner will be ready in about 15 minutes.

Four 7- to 8-ounce salmon fillets, skinned

$\frac{1}{2}$ teaspoon kosher salt

$\frac{1}{4}$ teaspoon freshly ground black pepper

2 tablespoons extra-virgin olive oil

Herbed White Beans

3 tablespoons extra-virgin olive oil

4 garlic cloves, chopped

$\frac{1}{4}$ teaspoon hot red pepper flakes

One 19-ounce can cannellini (white kidney) beans, drained and rinsed

One 14$\frac{1}{2}$-ounce can chopped tomatoes in juice

2 teaspoons chopped fresh rosemary, plus additional for garnish, optional

Kosher salt and freshly ground black pepper to taste

1. Position a rack in the center of the oven and preheat the oven to 400°F. Lightly oil a baking sheet.

2. Season the salmon with the salt and pepper. Place the fillets skinned side down on the baking sheet and generously brush with the oil. Bake until the salmon looks barely opaque with a tinge of rose color in the center when prodded with the tip of a knife, about 15 minutes.

3. Meanwhile, make the beans. Combine the oil, garlic, and red pepper flakes in a medium saucepan over low heat. Cook slowly until the garlic is golden, about 5 minutes. Add the beans, tomatoes with their juices, ½ cup water, and rosemary. Bring to a simmer. Reduce the heat to medium-low and simmer to blend the flavors, about 5 minutes. Season with salt and pepper. Cover the beans and keep warm.

4. Spoon an equal amount of the beans into soup bowls. Top with the salmon, sprinkle with more rosemary, if desired, and serve.

salmon fillets with black olive crust

MAKES 4 SERVINGS

The rich flavor of salmon can stand up to pretty strong partners, like this black olive crust. The result is a boldly seasoned dish that has a lot of fans in our family. Add other ingredients to the salad as you see fit—sliced cucumbers and garbanzo beans.

Black Olive Vinaigrette

⅓ cup **Black Olive Pesto (page 189)**

¼ cup **balsamic vinegar**

¼ cup **water**

1 tablespoon **fresh lime juice**

1 teaspoon **honey**

½ cup **extra-virgin olive oil**

Four 7- to 8-ounce salmon fillets, skinned

½ cup **Black Olive Pesto (page 189)**

6 tablespoons **Garlic Aioli (page 140), optional**

½ pound **mixed baby greens (mesclun)**

1 small **red onion, sliced into thin half-moons**

1 pint **red grape tomatoes**

1. To make the vinaigrette, combine the pesto, vinegar, water, lime juice, and honey in a blender. With the machine running, slowly add the oil. Set aside while cooking the salmon.

2. Position a rack in the center of the oven and preheat the oven to 350°F. Lightly oil a baking sheet.

3. Spread the flesh (not the skin) side of each fillet with 2 tablespoons of pesto. If using, spread 1½ tablespoons of aioli on top of the pesto. Place the salmon on the baking sheet. Bake until the aioli is golden brown and the salmon looks barely opaque with a tinge of rose color when flaked in the center with the tip of a sharp knife, about 15 minutes.

4. Toss the greens, onion, and tomato with the vinaigrette. Arrange equal amounts of the salad on 4 dinner plates and top each with a salmon fillet.

crispy sole with parsley and chives

MAKES 4 TO 6 SERVINGS

Three matzo products (meal, flour, and farfel) combine to make an incredibly crisp coating for fish fillets. Don't skimp on the oil and butter, or the crust could scorch.

Matzo Crust

²/₃ **cup matzo meal**

²/₃ **cup matzo flour**

²/₃ **cup matzo farfel**

4 tablespoons extra-virgin olive oil

4 tablespoons unsalted butter, cut up

Four 7-ounce sole fillets

¹/₂ **teaspoon kosher salt**

¹/₄ **teaspoon freshly ground black pepper**

¹/₃ **cup matzo flour**

2 large eggs

2 tablespoons chopped fresh parsley

2 tablespoons chopped fresh chives

Lemon wedges for serving

1. To make the matzo crust, mix the matzo meal, matzo flour, and matzo farfel in a shallow dish.

2. Heat the oil and butter together in a very large skillet over medium heat until the butter melts and the mixture is very hot, but not smoking. Meanwhile, season the fish with salt and pepper. Place the plain matzo flour in another shallow dish. Beat the eggs and 2 tablespoons water in a third shallow dish. Dip each fillet in flour to coat and shake off the excess flour. Dip in the eggs to coat, then coat with the matzo crust, pressing it gently to adhere.

3. Place the fillets in the skillet. Cook, turning once, until the crust is crisp and golden, about 5 minutes.

4. Using a slotted spatula, transfer the fish to 4 dinner plates. Mix the parsley and chives, and sprinkle over the fish. Serve hot with the lemon wedges.

cornflake-crusted sea bass with corn and black bean salsa

MAKES 4 SERVINGS

My nana taught me that cornflakes have an active life in the kitchen outside of the cereal bowl. They make a great coating for fish, as demonstrated here by these crunchy sea bass fillets. And get to know panko, those super-crispy Japanese bread crumbs. These sweet fillets with the crackling, fun crust may be a way to get the kids to eat more fish.

Corn and Black Bean Salsa

1 cup fresh or defrosted frozen corn kernels

One 15- to 19-ounce can black beans, drained and rinsed

½ cup finely chopped red onion

⅓ cup seeded and finely chopped red bell pepper

¼ cup extra-virgin olive oil

¼ cup chopped fresh cilantro

3 tablespoons fresh lime juice

1 jalapeño, seeded and finely chopped

Kosher salt and freshly ground black pepper to taste

Cornflake-Crusted Sea Bass

½ cup all-purpose flour

2 large eggs

¾ cup crushed cornflakes (see Note) or use store-bought cornflake crumbs

¼ cup panko (Japanese bread crumbs, see Note, page 69)

1 tablespoon chili powder

Four 6-ounce sea bass fillets

½ teaspoon kosher salt

¼ teaspoon freshly ground black pepper

3 tablespoons extra-virgin olive oil

1. To make the salsa, combine all the ingredients in a medium bowl, and season with the salt and pepper. Cover and set aside while preparing the fish, but preferably an hour or so. (The salsa can be prepared up to 1 day ahead, covered and refrigerated. Return to room temperature before serving.)

2. To prepare the sea bass, spread the flour in a shallow dish or plate. Lightly beat the eggs with 1 tablespoon water in another dish. Mix the cornflake crumbs, panko, and chili powder in a third dish. Season the fish lightly with the salt and pepper. One at a time, coat one side (the meaty side, not the skin side) of each fillet in the flour. Dip the floured side of the fish in the eggs, then in the crumb coating, patting on the coating to help it adhere. Place the fillets, coated side up, on a baking sheet and refrigerate to set the crust while preheating the oven.

3. Position a rack in the center of the oven and preheat the oven to 350°F. Heat the oil in a large ovenproof skillet over medium-high heat until the oil is very hot but not smoking. Add the fish fillets, coated sides down, and cook, just until the underside is crisp and golden brown, about 2 minutes. Turn the fillets, place in the oven, and bake until the fish is barely opaque in the center (use the tip of a small sharp knife to check a fillet), about 8 minutes. Transfer each fillet to a dinner plate and top with a generous spoonful of the salsa. Serve immediately.

NOTE Place the cornflakes in a zippered plastic bag and roll with a rolling pin until they are evenly and coarsely crushed. You can also find crushed cornflakes next to the dried bread crumbs in some supermarkets.

herbed sea bass with orange-rosemary butter

MAKES 4 SERVINGS

This ultrasimple fish entrée is all about the fresh flavor and seductive aroma of herbs. The sea bass fillets are encrusted in herbs, then an orange-scented rosemary compound butter goes on top to create a casual sauce. Snapper or grouper fillets would also be sensational substitutes for the sea bass. In addition to the recipe below, this butter does wonderful things melted over other fish fillets or cooked vegetables, such as asparagus or broccoli.

Four 6-ounce sea bass fillets, skinned

3 tablespoons extra-virgin olive oil

½ teaspoon kosher salt

¼ teaspoon freshly ground black pepper

2 tablespoons each chopped fresh rosemary, parsley, thyme, and basil or 4 tablespoons each parsley and basil

6 tablespoons Orange-Rosemary Butter (recipe follows), cut into 4 pats

1. Position a rack in the center of the oven and preheat to 400°F. Brush the fish on both sides with the oil. Season with the salt and pepper. Spread the herbs on a plate. Dip the flesh side of each fillet in the herbs to coat.

2. Heat a large, ovenproof nonstick skillet over medium-high heat. Add the fish, herbed sides down, and cook until lightly browned, about 6 minutes. Turn the fish. Place in the oven and bake just until the fish looks opaque when flaked in the center with the tip of a sharp knife, about 2 minutes. Just as the fish comes out of the oven, place a pat of the butter on each fillet.

3. Using a slotted spatula, transfer each fillet to a dinner plate. Serve immediately.

Orange-Rosemary Butter

MAKES ABOUT 1 CUP

1 cup (2 sticks) unsalted butter, softened

Zest of 2 oranges

¼ cup fresh orange juice

1½ teaspoons finely chopped fresh rosemary

½ teaspoon kosher or sea salt

¼ teaspoon freshly ground black pepper

1. Using an electric mixer on medium speed (I prefer a standing mixer with a paddle blade for this recipe, but a hand mixer will work, too), beat the butter in a medium bowl until it is light and fluffy, about 2 minutes. Add the orange zest and juice, rosemary, salt, and pepper and mix well.

2. Place an 18-inch square of plastic wrap on your work surface. Scrape the butter out onto the wrap, about 2 inches from the bottom edge, shaping the butter into a rough strip about 12 inches long and 2 inches wide. Fold the bottom edge of the plastic wrap over to cover the butter. Roll up the plastic wrap to shape the butter into a cylinder. Pick up the cylinder by the two ends of plastic wrap. Twist the ends of the wrap in opposite directions, and it will tighten to shape the butter into a compact log (see photographs on page 131). Refrigerate the butter until it is firm, at least 2 hours. (The butter can be refrigerated for up to 1 week. To freeze the butter, wrap the log, still in the plastic wrap, in aluminum foil and freeze for up to 3 months.)

Compound Butters

Compound butters are nothing more than unsalted butter that has been flavored, frequently with herbs and spices. By investing just a few minutes of time, you can have a cup of beautifully seasoned butter, ready to melt over vegetables or fish. Because the fat in the butter surrounds the herbs and other ingredients to keep out air, the flavors remain fresh and the colors bright. With the help of plastic wrap, the butter is shaped into a log, which can then be over-wrapped in aluminum foil and frozen for a few months. I encourage you keep a trove of the Orange-Rosemary Butter (this page); Chile, Lime, and Cilantro Butter (page 131); and Sun-Dried Tomato, Olive, and Thyme Butter (page 209) in your freezer, too.

brook trout with chile, lime, and cilantro butter

MAKES 4 SERVINGS

The mild flesh of brook trout can withstand some spicing up, and this hot and spicy compound butter fits the bill. Melt a pat of the leftover butter over grilled tuna steaks, sautéed grouper or sea bass or use it to dress up steamed vegetables.

¼ cup extra-virgin olive oil

Four 6-ounce brook trout fillets

½ teaspoon kosher salt

¼ teaspoon freshly ground black pepper

½ cup all-purpose flour

6 tablespoons Chile, Lime, and Cilantro Butter (recipe follows), cut into 4 pats

1. Position a rack in the center of the oven and preheat to 400°F.

2. Heat the oil in a large skillet over medium-high heat. Season the fillets with salt and pepper. Spread the flour in a shallow bowl. Dip both sides of each fillet into the flour and shake off the excess. Add to the skillet, flesh sides down, and cook until the undersides are golden brown, about 6 minutes. Turn the fish. Place in the oven and bake just until the fish looks opaque when flaked in the center with the tip of a sharp knife, about 2 minutes. Just as the fish comes out of the oven, place a pat of the butter on each fillet.

3. Using a slotted spatula, transfer each fillet to a dinner plate. Serve immediately.

Olive Oil

Some cooks warn against sautéing with extra-virgin olive oil because it has a low smoke point (the threshold where the oil smokes, which alters its flavor). Well, you'll have to get the oil very, very hot before it smokes. Besides, green-hued extra-virgin oil has much better flavor than golden pure olive oil. So, if cooking is all about flavor—use extra-virgin oil. But plain oil is really okay for sautéing, if you insist.

Chile, Lime, and Cilantro Butter

MAKES 1 CUP

In addition to its traditional uses on fish and vegetables, toss some of this butter with egg noodles and some freshly grated Parmesan cheese for a great dairy side dish.

1 cup (2 sticks) unsalted butter, softened

3 serrano chiles, seeded and minced

¼ cup chopped fresh cilantro

Grated zest of 1 lime

2 tablespoons fresh lime juice

½ teaspoon kosher or sea salt

¼ teaspoon freshly ground black pepper

1. Using an electric mixer on medium speed (I prefer a standing mixer with a paddle blade for this recipe, but a hand mixer will work, too), beat the butter in a medium bowl until it is light and fluffy, about 2 minutes. Add the chiles, cilantro, lime zest, lime juice, salt, and pepper and mix well.

2. Place an 18-inch square of plastic wrap on your work surface. Scrape the butter out onto the wrap, about 2 inches from the bottom edge, shaping the butter into a rough strip about 12 inches long and 2 inches wide. Fold the bottom edge of the plastic wrap over to cover the butter. Roll up the plastic wrap to shape the butter into a cylinder. Pick up the cylinder by the two ends of plastic wrap. Twist the ends of the wrap, and it will tighten to shape the butter into a compact log (see below). Refrigerate the butter until it is firm, at least 2 hours. (The butter can be made up to 1 week ahead, refrigerated or freeze for up to 3 months.)

spicy batter-fried tilapia with zhug mayonnaise

MAKES 4 SERVINGS

Think of this as Jewish fish and chips without the chips (or make the Spicy Oven Fries on page 202). Explain to the kids that zhug is not the name of a cartoon character, but the most popular spice mixture in Yemenite cooking, a hot blend of parsley, cilantro, chiles, and spices. It turns store-bought mayo into a condiment from heaven. Stir leftover zhug into soups and stews, or spread it thinly on toasted pita bread as a sinus-clearing appetizer.

Zhug

3 jalapeños, seeded

4 garlic cloves, crushed under a knife and peeled

1 ripe plum tomato, quartered lengthwise

½ cup packed fresh parsley leaves

½ cup packed fresh cilantro leaves

2 tablespoons fresh lemon juice

1 tablespoon ground cumin

1 tablespoon curry powder

1 teaspoon ground turmeric

½ teaspoon kosher salt

½ teaspoon freshly ground black pepper

2½ tablespoons extra-virgin olive oil

1 cup mayonnaise

Batter

1⅓ cups all-purpose flour

1 teaspoon sweet Hungarian paprika

½ teaspoon baking powder

1 cup beer

Tilapia

2 pounds tilapia or cod fillets, cut into 1-inch pieces

2 teaspoons freshly ground black pepper

¾ teaspoon ground cumin

¾ teaspoon ground coriander

¾ teaspoon fine sea or kosher salt

Vegetable oil, for deep-frying

½ cup all-purpose flour

½ cup cornstarch

1. To make the zhug, fit a food processor with the metal chopping blade. With the machine running, drop the jalapeños and garlic through the feed tube to finely chop them. Add the tomato, parsley, and cilantro and pulse to finely chop the herbs. Mix the lemon juice, cumin, curry powder, turmeric, salt, and pepper in a small bowl. Add to the food processor. With the machine running, slowly pour in the olive oil and process to make a coarse paste. You will have about $1\frac{2}{3}$ cups of zhug.

2. Stir 6 tablespoons or so of the zhug into the mayonnaise to taste. Cover and refrigerate until ready to use. (The mayonnaise can be prepared up to 2 weeks ahead, covered, and refrigerated. The zhug can be refrigerated in a covered container, with a thin film of olive oil poured over the surface, for up to 3 weeks.)

3. To make the batter, sift the flour, paprika, and baking powder into a large bowl. Add the beer and whisk until barely smooth. Set aside to rest for at least 15 minutes and up to 1 hour.

4. To prepare the tilapia, mix the pepper, cumin, coriander, and salt in a small bowl. Season the fish all over with the spices mixture. Let stand for 15 minutes. (Do not refrigerate, as ice-cold food will make the deep-frying oil bubble up.)

5. Preheat the oven to 200°F. Line a baking sheet with a double thickness of paper towels. Pour enough oil to come 3 inches up the sides of a large, wide saucepan or Dutch oven and heat over high heat until a deep-frying thermometer reads 360°F.

6. Mix the flour and cornstarch in a medium bowl. In batches, without crowding, dip each piece of fish into the flour mixture, and then into the beer batter. Deep-fry until crisp and golden, 2 to 3 minutes. Using a wire skimmer or a slotted spoon, transfer the fish to the baking sheet and keep warm in the oven while deep-frying the remaining fish. Serve hot with the mayonnaise passed on the side as a dip.

tilapia teriyaki with stir-fried asian vegetables

MAKES 4 SERVINGS

I learned how to make this easy teriyaki sauce during my years cooking at a Japanese restaurant in New York. Keep a supply in your refrigerator, and you'll be able to create a variety of fast stir-fries at a moment's notice. As there is no protein in the sauce to encourage bacteria growth, it will keep refrigerated for weeks. Here, I use it with tilapia and a quick sauté of snow peas, red peppers, and shiitake mushrooms. But there's no reason why you couldn't swap the tilapia with salmon fillets or boneless, skinless chicken breasts and whatever vegetables are handy. Kids love this dish's gingery, slightly sweet sauce, and adults will appreciate its low-fat profile.

Teriyaki Sauce

1 cup mirin (see Note) or sweet white wine

1 cup soy sauce

2 tablespoons sugar

1½ teaspoons finely chopped fresh ginger

1 teaspoons ketchup

1 small garlic clove, finely chopped

2 teaspoons cornstarch

2 tablespoons canola oil

Six 6- to 7-ounce tilapia fillets

½ teaspoon kosher salt

¼ teaspoon freshly ground black pepper

½ cup flour

1 tablespoon finely chopped fresh ginger

2 garlic cloves, finely chopped

3 ounces snow peas, cut in halves on the bias

1 red bell pepper, cored, seeded, and cut into ¼-inch-wide strips

3 ounces shiitake mushrooms, stems removed, caps cut into ¼-inch-wide strips

1. To make the sauce, bring the mirin, soy sauce, sugar, ginger, ketchup, and garlic to a boil in a medium saucepan over medium heat, stirring often. Sprinkle the cornstarch over 2 tablespoons cold water in a small bowl and stir to dissolve. Stir into the simmering sauce and cook just until thickened. Set aside. (The sauce can be cooled and refrigerated in a covered container for up to 2 months.)

2. Heat 1 tablespoon oil in a very large nonstick skillet over medium-high heat. Season the fillets with salt and pepper. Spread the flour on a plate. Dip the fillets on both sides in flour and shake off the excess. Place in the skillet and cook until the underside is lightly browned, about $2\frac{1}{2}$ minutes. Turn and brown the other side, about $2\frac{1}{2}$ minutes more. Transfer the fish to a platter and tent with aluminum foil to keep warm. Wipe out the skillet with paper towels.

3. Add the remaining 1 tablespoon of oil to the skillet and heat over high heat. Add the ginger and garlic and stir until fragrant, about 30 seconds. Add the snow peas, bell pepper, and mushrooms, and stir-fry until crisp-tender, about $2\frac{1}{2}$ minutes. Add 3 tablespoons of the teriyaki sauce, and stir until heated through. Heap the vegetables on the fish.

4. Serve hot, with the remaining sauce on the side, if desired.

NOTE Mirin is a sweet, syrupy rice wine used in Japanese cooking, and kosher brands can be found at many Asian markets. A sweet wine, such as Riesling, is an acceptable substitute.

tilapia with classic francese sauce

MAKES 4 SERVINGS

This restaurant favorite, with lightly battered fish in a tart lemon-butter sauce, is a good recipe for home cooks who love simple, straightforward flavors.

Four 6- to 7-ounce tilapia fillets
$\frac{1}{2}$ teaspoon kosher salt
$\frac{1}{4}$ teaspoon freshly ground black pepper
$\frac{1}{3}$ cup all-purpose flour
4 large eggs
$\frac{1}{4}$ cup extra-virgin olive oil

Francese Sauce
2 garlic cloves or 1 shallot, minced
$\frac{3}{4}$ cup dry white wine, such as Chardonnay
$\frac{1}{4}$ cup fresh lemon juice
6 tablespoons ($\frac{3}{4}$ stick) unsalted butter, cut into $\frac{1}{2}$-inch cubes, chilled
2 tablespoons chopped fresh parsley
Kosher salt and freshly ground black pepper to taste

1. Season the fillets with the salt and pepper. Place the flour in a shallow dish. Crack the eggs into another shallow dish and beat well.

2. Heat the oil in a very large skillet over medium heat until the oil is very hot but not smoking. One fillet at a time, dip the fish in the flour to coat, shake off the excess flour, then dip into the beaten egg to coat. Place in the skillet and cook until the undersides of the fillets are golden brown, about 2 minutes. Turn the fillets.

3. Scatter the garlic around the fillets in the skillet and cook just until the garlic softens, about 1 minute. Add the wine and lemon juice. Simmer about 2 minutes. Using a long, slotted spatula, transfer the fish to a platter.

4. Remove the skillet from the heat. Whisk in the butter, a few cubes at a time, shaking the skillet at the same time to help emulsify the sauce. Whisk in the parsley and season with salt and pepper. Spoon the sauce over the fish and serve immediately.

tuna-stuffed peppers

MAKES 6 SERVINGS

There is a rule in some areas of Italy about not cooking cheese with fish, but as no such rule exists in my cooking, stuff these peppers with tuna and three kinds of cheese. You'll love it!

3 medium bell peppers, preferably 1 each red, yellow, and green

One 6-ounce can tuna in oil or water, drained

½ cup part-skim or whole-milk ricotta cheese

1⅔ cups shredded mozzarella cheese

1 tablespoon freshly grated Parmesan cheese

3 anchovy fillets packed in oil, drained and finely chopped

2 large eggs plus 1 large egg yolk

3 tablespoons chopped fresh parsley

1 tablespoon chopped fresh sage, optional

1 teaspoon dried oregano

¼ teaspoon kosher salt

¼ teaspoon freshly ground black pepper

½ cup dried Italian-seasoned bread crumbs

1. Position a rack in the upper third of the oven and preheat the oven to 350°F. Lightly oil a 15 × 10-inch baking pan.

2. Cut each pepper in half lengthwise. Remove and discard the seeds and ribs, but the stems can remain as decorations.

3. Flake the tuna well in a medium bowl. Add the ricotta, mozzarella, Parmesan, and anchovies and mix to combine. Whisk the eggs, egg yolk, parsley, sage (if using), oregano, salt, and pepper in a small bowl. Add to the tuna mixture and fold in with a rubber spatula.

4. Fill each pepper with an equal amount of the tuna filling. Place the bread crumbs in a small bowl. One at a time, invert the peppers into the bread crumbs to coat the filling with crumbs. Place the peppers, crumbed sides up, in the pan.

5. Bake until the tops are golden and the peppers soften, 25 to 30 minutes. Serve hot, or cool until warm.

blackened tuna with marinated cucumber salad

MAKES 4 SERVINGS

The cool and crisp cucumber salad, which is almost a pickle, plays off the hot and spicy tuna. Two things to watch out for when "blackening" food: First, use a heavy skillet—a well-seasoned cast-iron one is ideal. Also, don't try this recipe unless you have a strong kitchen range hood, as the spice crust creates a good amount of smoke. I also apply the technique to thin cuts of chicken and beef, so I find it convenient to mix up a batch of blackening spices and store it for future meals, and I encourage you to do the same.

Marinated Cucumber Salad

¼ cup fresh lemon juice

¼ cup white distilled vinegar

1½ tablespoons kosher salt

¼ cup extra-virgin olive oil

2 seedless English cucumbers, unpeeled, halved lengthwise, and thinly sliced into half-moons

1 medium red bell pepper, cored, seeded, and cut into thin matchsticks

1 small red onion, halved lengthwise and thinly sliced into half-moons

¼ cup chopped fresh parsley

2 tablespoons canola oil

½ cup Blackened Spice Blend (recipe follows)

Four 8-ounce skinless tuna steaks

1. To make the cucumber salad, whisk the lemon juice, vinegar, and salt in a large bowl to dissolve the salt. Whisk in the oil. Add the cucumbers, red pepper, onion, and parsley, and mix well. Cover and refrigerate for at least 1 hour and up to 4 hours.

2. Heat the canola oil in a large, heavy (preferably cast-iron) skillet over high heat until the oil is very hot but not smoking. Sprinkle 2 tablespoons of the spice blend on both sides of each tuna steak. Add the tuna to the skillet and cook until the undersides are very well browned, about 3 minutes. Turn and brown the other sides.

3. Transfer each tuna steak to a dinner plate. Using a slotted spoon, serve a portion of the cucumber salad next to each steak. Serve immediately.

Blackened Spice Blend

MAKES ABOUT 1¹/₃ CUPS

This is one of the all-time great spice mixtures. My version isn't just peppery hot, but balanced with some warm, fragrant spices like cinnamon, coriander, nutmeg, and cloves.

⅓ cup plus 2 tablespoons freshly ground black pepper

¼ cup gumbo filé (see Note)

3 tablespoons kosher salt

2 tablespoons freshly grated nutmeg

1 tablespoon plus 1 teaspoon ground cardamom

1 tablespoon ground cinnamon

1 tablespoon ground cloves

1¼ teaspoons ground coriander

1 teaspoon hot red pepper flakes

1 teaspoon ground cayenne pepper

Whisk the pepper, filé, salt, nutmeg, cardamom, cinnamon, cloves, coridander, red pepper flakes, and cayenne to combine well. Transfer to a covered jar and store in a cool dry place for up to 6 months.

NOTE Gumbo filé is the ground bark of the sassafras tree. When heated in liquid-based soups and stews, it acts as a thickener, but it also lends a musky flavor to this spice blend. If you can't find it, you can leave it out of this recipe. A kosher version is available from www.chefjeffgourmet.com, 1-888-562-4331.

tuna-basil burgers with aioli and arugula

MAKES 6 SERVINGS

The Nathans enjoy a good beef burger as much as the next family, but when you put one of these babies in front of us, we're in heaven. First of all, anything with garlic in it has our vote, and aioli, the Provençal mayonnaise, is loaded with the stuff. As for the tuna, watch out for a couple of things. First you really must chop the tuna by hand with a heavy, sharp knife—with a food processor, it is too difficult to control the size of the pieces. And although the olive oil in the chopped tuna helps keep the burgers moist, don't cook the burgers past the medium-rare stage.

Garlic Aioli

1 tablespoon fresh lemon juice

$\frac{1}{8}$ teaspoon crushed saffron threads, optional

1 cup mayonnaise

3 garlic cloves, minced, then sprinkled with kosher salt and mashed to a paste

Kosher salt and freshly ground black pepper to taste

Tuna-Basil Burgers

3 pounds skinless tuna steaks

$\frac{3}{4}$ cup plus 3 tablespoons extra-virgin olive oil

$\frac{1}{2}$ cup coarsely chopped fresh basil

8 garlic cloves, minced

4 anchovy fillets, minced

Kosher salt and freshly ground black pepper to taste

6 hamburger buns, toasted

2 cups fresh arugula, well rinsed

1 large, ripe beefsteak tomato, sliced

Lemon wedges, for serving

1. To make the aioli, mix the lemon juice and saffron, if using, in a small bowl. Set aside for 15 minutes to infuse the lemon juice with the saffron flavor and color. Mix the mayonnaise, garlic paste, and saffron mixture in a medium bowl and season with salt and pepper. Cover and refrigerate until ready to serve.

2. To make the tuna burgers, place the tuna on a chopping board and chop finely with a large sharp knife; do not use a food processor. Mix the chopped tuna, ¾ cup of oil, basil, garlic, and anchovies in a medium bowl. Season with salt and pepper. Oil your hands, and shape the tuna into six 3- to 4-inch-wide patties.

3. Heat the remaining 3 tablespoons oil in a very large skillet over high heat (you can use less oil if you have a nonstick skillet). Add the tuna patties and cook until the underside is browned, about 2 minutes. Turn and brown the other side for 2 minutes more for rare tuna burgers.

4. Serve the tuna burgers on the buns, topped with a dollop of aioli. Pass the arugula, sliced tomato, lemon wedges, and remaining aioli on the side.

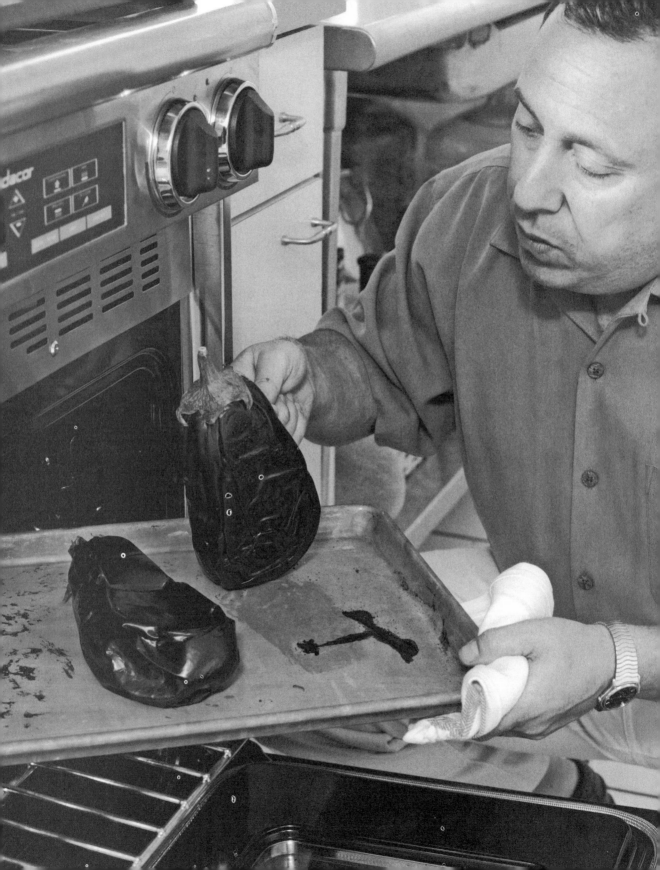

vegetable main courses

How many times do parents invoke the command "Eat your vegetables!" to their children? Now, I'm not saying that Ali and I never had to use these words, but I think that we did so less often than other parents. The trick is to incorporate an exciting and colorful array of vegetables into the family menu, not just as side dishes, but also as main courses.

Vegetarian cooking is hardly a recent invention. Cuisines all around the globe have been cooking without meat for eons, and their traditions influence today's meatless family suppers. And let's not forget Shavuot, the holiday that always features dairy meals, celebrating the Biblical description of Israel as "the land of milk and honey."

I've included dishes that lend themselves especially well to vegetarian suppers: kugels and latkes. I'm always looking for ways to bring new life to these old favorites. For a sweet kugel, you couldn't do much better than my mascarpone and citrus version on page 154. The Mashed Potato and Vegetable Kugel on page 156 is an example of the savory variety. And while every family has treasured a potato latke recipe (probably handed down from Nana), why not try my Provençale-flavored version (page 148) or the falafel-inspired ones (page 146)?

This selection of vegetarian recipes offers a world of flavors, from Italy to Spain to Eastern Europe. I'm sure Nana would heartily approve of Wild Mushroom Kasha (page 150), which deliciously combines new and old cooking sensibilities.

stuffed eggplant with peppers, cheese, and pine nuts

MAKES 6 SERVINGS

There are a lot of things that you can use to stuff eggplant, and ground meat does not have to be one of them. This version fills eggplant shells to the brim with sweet peppers, cheese, basil, and pine nuts for crunch. A stick of butter to cook the vegetables may seem excessive, but eggplant has a tendency to soak up fat during cooking. You could use all olive oil, but I like the flavor of the butter here.

½ cup pine nuts, toasted (see Note)

3 medium eggplants, about 1 pound each, rinsed and patted dry

8 tablespoons (1 stick) unsalted butter

3 tablespoons olive oil

2 medium onions, finely chopped

1 green bell pepper, cored, seeded, and finely chopped

1 red bell pepper, cored, seeded, and finely chopped

3 garlic cloves, chopped

3 ripe plum tomatoes, cut into ½-inch dice

2 cups (½ pound) shredded Havarti or mozzarella cheese

2 tablespoons chopped fresh basil

Kosher salt and freshly ground black pepper to taste

1. Position a rack in the center of the oven and preheat the oven to 350°F. Lightly oil a rimmed baking sheet.

2. Cut each eggplant in half lengthwise. Using a large spoon, scoop out the flesh from each eggplant half, leaving a ¼-inch-thick shell. Chop the eggplant flesh into ½-inch dice.

3. Heat the butter and oil together in a large skillet over medium-high heat until the butter melts. Add the onions, chopped eggplant, green and red bell peppers, and garlic. Cook, stirring often, until the eggplant is tender, about 10 minutes. Add the tomatoes and cook until they soften, about 3 minutes more. Remove from the heat. Stir in the cheese, basil, and reserved pine nuts. Season with salt and pepper. Fill each eggplant half with an equal amount of the filling and arrange them on the baking sheet.

4. Bake until the eggplant shells are tender when pierced with the tip of a knife, about 30 minutes. Serve hot.

NOTE To toast pine nuts, heat an empty medium skillet over medium heat. Add the pine nuts and cook, stirring often, until they are toasted, about 3 minutes. Transfer to a plate and cool.

falafel latkes with spicy chili sauce

MAKES ABOUT 24 LATKES

When you take a favorite of Israeli cooking and cross it with an icon of the Jewish-American kitchen, what do you get? Falafel latkes! Talk about the best of both worlds. . . . I like to serve these next to a heap of Red and Yellow Israeli Salad (page 57). If your family loves latkes as much as mine, you might want to get in the habit of cooking extras for freezing. Just be sure that the pancakes are cooked all the way through, as any uncooked portions will turn brown when frozen. Cool the latkes completely, wrap each one in plastic wrap, and then store in a freezer bag. To reheat, unwrap and place on a baking sheet, and bake in a 400°F oven until crisped, about 10 minutes.

Spicy Chili Sauce

$\frac{1}{4}$ cup fresh lemon juice, or more as needed

1 tablespoon chili powder

$\frac{2}{3}$ cup sour cream

$\frac{1}{2}$ cup mayonnaise

Kosher salt and freshly ground black pepper to taste

Latkes

1 large baking potato (8 ounces), such as Burbank or russet, peeled

$\frac{1}{2}$ medium red onion

2 garlic cloves

One 15- to 19-ounce can garbanzo beans (chickpeas), drained

$\frac{1}{2}$ cup packed cilantro leaves

$1\frac{1}{2}$ teaspoons ground cumin

2 teaspoons kosher salt

$\frac{1}{4}$ teaspoon freshly ground black pepper

1 large egg, beaten

2 tablespoons all-purpose flour

Olive oil, for frying, as needed

1. To make the sauce, whisk together the lemon juice and chili powder, fold in the sour cream and mayonnaise, and season with salt and pepper. If the sauce seems too thick, thin with more lemon juice. Set aside while making the latkes.

2. Position a rack in the center of the oven and preheat the oven to 200°F. Line a baking sheet with paper towels. Fit a food processor with the shredding blade. Shred the potato, onion, and garlic into the work bowl. A handful at a time, squeeze the excess moisture from the potato mixture, and transfer to another bowl.

3. Fit the food processor with the metal chopping blade (don't bother to clean the processor). Add the garbanzo beans, cilantro, cumin, salt, and pepper and process until the beans are puréed. Scrape into the shredded potatoes, add the egg and flour, and mix.

4. Add enough oil to a large, deep skillet to come ½ inch up the sides. Do not skimp! Heat over medium-high heat until very hot but not smoking. In batches, without crowding, and using about ¼ cup of the potato mixture for each pancake, carefully add the mixture to the oil, spreading it with a spoon to make 3-inch pancakes. Fry, turning once, until deep golden brown on both sides. Use a slotted spatula to transfer to the baking sheet. Serve immediately or keep warm in the oven while making the remaining pancakes. Drain off any excess liquid that forms in the bowl as you make subsequent batches.

5. Serve the latkes hot with the sauce passed on the side.

provençale potato latkes
with roasted red pepper relish

MAKES ABOUT 20 LATKES, 5 TO 6 SERVINGS

I'll never turn down a plate of well-made plain latkes, but I really enjoy upping the ante by adding more flavors to the potato pancakes. This time around, I use garlic and herbs, and top the crisp discs with a roasted pepper relish. Leftover relish makes a mean condiment for a goat cheese sandwich.

Roasted Red Pepper Relish

Two 14-ounce cans roasted red peppers, drained and cut into $\frac{1}{2}$-inch dice (about 1$\frac{3}{4}$ cups)

1 cup pitted Kalamata olives, coarsely chopped

$\frac{1}{3}$ cup chopped fresh herbs, such as rosemary, thyme, basil, and oregano in any combination

2 tablespoons coarsely chopped roasted garlic

2 tablespoons extra-virgin olive oil

1 tablespoon balsamic vinegar

Kosher salt and freshly ground black pepper to taste

Provençale Latkes

4 large russet potatoes, peeled (2 pounds)

1 pound yellow onions (2 large)

2 large eggs, beaten

$\frac{1}{3}$ cup all-purpose flour

2 tablespoons chopped fresh parsley

4 garlic cloves, finely chopped

$\frac{1}{2}$ teaspoon dried basil

$\frac{1}{2}$ teaspoon dried oregano

$\frac{1}{2}$ teaspoon dried thyme

$\frac{1}{4}$ teaspoon fennel seed, toasted, optional

2 teaspoons kosher salt

$\frac{1}{4}$ teaspoon freshly ground black pepper

Olive oil, for frying

1. Position a rack in the center of the oven and preheat the oven to 200°F. Line a baking sheet with paper towels.

2. To make the relish, combine all of the ingredients and season with the salt and pepper. Let stand at room temperature while making the latkes. (The relish can be made up to 5 days ahead, covered, and refrigerated. Bring to room temperature before serving.)

3. Using the large holes of a box grater or the grating disk of a food processor, alternately grate the potatoes and onions into a work bowl (this provides better distribution of the onions). Using your hands, squeeze out as much moisture as you can from the potato mixture. Add the eggs, flour, parsley, garlic, basil, oregano, thyme, fennel (if using), and the salt and pepper, and mix well.

4. Add enough oil to a large, deep skillet to come ½ inch up the sides. Do not skimp! Heat over medium-high heat until very hot but not smoking. In batches, without crowding, and using about ¼ cup of the potato mixture for each latke, carefully add the mixture to the oil, spreading it with the back of a spoon to make 3-inch pancakes. Fry, turning once, until deep golden brown on both sides. Using a slotted spatula, transfer the latkes to the baking sheet. Serve immediately or keep warm in the oven while making the remaining latkes. Drain off any excess liquid that forms in the bowl as you make subsequent batches.

5. Serve hot with the relish.

DAIRY VARIATION

Add ⅔ cup crumbled goat cheese to the relish. Gently fold the cheese into the relish so the cheese doesn't break down.

wild mushroom kasha

MAKES 6 TO 8 SERVINGS

My family gives this recipe a workout. Packed with lots of mushrooms, we like it as a vegetarian main course, served with a hearty green salad. When the weather is hot, we'll let it cool to room temperature—it's still good, even without a dressing. We use it as the base for some pretty spectacular kasha varnishkes (see the variation below). Or it can be used as a side dish for a holiday meal, in which case it will serve up to twelve guests. Use medium-grain kasha for the best texture.

3 tablespoons olive oil

1 small red onion, chopped

6 garlic cloves, chopped

1 pound assorted mushrooms, such as pleurotte, cremini, and shiitake caps, sliced

One 13-ounce box medium-grain kasha

2 large egg whites

4 cups Vegetable Broth (page 44) or vegetable bouillon

1 tablespoon soy sauce

2 bay leaves

1 teaspoon kosher salt

¼ teaspoon freshly ground black pepper

2 tablespoons chopped fresh thyme or 1 teaspoon dried thyme

1. Heat the oil in a large saucepan over medium heat. Add the onion and garlic and cook, stirring often, until the onion is translucent, about 6 minutes. Add the mushrooms and cook until they release their juices, about 5 minutes.

2. Meanwhile, mix the kasha and egg whites in a medium bowl to evenly coat the kasha grains with the whites. Heat a large empty nonstick skillet over medium heat. Add the kasha and cook, stirring often, until the egg coating is dry, about 2 minutes. (This toasting step helps keep the cooked kasha grains separate and firm.)

3. Stir the kasha, broth, soy sauce, bay leaves, salt, and pepper into the saucepan with the mushrooms and bring to a boil over high heat. Reduce the heat to medium-low and cover tightly. Simmer until the kasha is tender and has absorbed the liquid, about 20 minutes.

4. Remove from the heat and fluff the kasha with a fork. Remove the bay leaves and stir in the thyme. Serve hot.

VARIATION: KASHA VARNISHKES WITH WILD MUSHROOMS

Cook 8 ounces bow-tie pasta (about 3 cups) in lightly salted boiling water until tender. Drain and stir into the cooked kasha. Makes 8 servings.

sicilian-style stuffed bell peppers

MAKES 4 SERVINGS

What's unusual about these stuffed bell peppers (well, unusual to American cooks, but probably not to Sicilians) is that they are filled with savory bread crumbs and not rice, ground meat, or others of the same-old–same-olds. With the classic combination of anchovy, raisins, and capers for a wonderfully sweet-and-salty-and-bitter interplay, they are equally great hot out of the oven or cooled to room temperature for a warm-weather entrée.

4 sweet bell peppers, either red, yellow, orange, or green

1 cup Italian-seasoned dry bread crumbs

⅓ cup plus 1 tablespoon golden raisins, plumped and drained (see opposite)

6 boneless anchovy fillets, finely chopped

¼ cup nonpareil capers, drained and rinsed

2 tablespoons chopped fresh parsley

2 tablespoons chopped fresh basil

1 cup extra-virgin olive oil, plus more as needed

Freshly ground black pepper to taste

½ cup canned tomato sauce, as needed

1. Position a rack in the center of the oven and preheat the oven to 400°F. Lightly oil a large baking sheet.

2. Trim the stems from the peppers. Cut each pepper in half lengthwise (or in thirds, if they are very large). Remove the seeds and large veins. Place the peppers skin side down on the baking sheet.

3. Mix the bread crumbs, raisins, anchovies, capers, parsley, and basil in a medium bowl. Add the oil and stir well to make a crumbly mixture with the texture of wet sand. Season with the pepper. (You won't need any salt, thanks to the anchovies.) Spread the crumb mixture in a thin layer onto the cut surface of each pepper. Drizzle each with about a teaspoon of oil and top each with 1 tablespoon of tomato sauce.

4. Bake until the peppers are wilted and the crumb filling is golden brown, about 25 minutes. Serve hot, or cool to room temperature.

DAIRY VARIATION

Add ¼ cup freshly grated Parmesan cheese to the bread crumbs.

Plumping Raisins

Raisins are dried grapes, right? When they come into contact with liquid, they soak it up, which can play havoc with your recipe. It is a much better idea to soak the raisins in water before using them. This step makes the soaked raisins nice and plump, which adds to the visual appeal of the dish, too. Also, dried, unhydrated raisins exposed to the heat of an oven could burn.

To plump raisins, place them in a small bowl and add enough warm water to cover them by about 1 inch. Let stand until they swell, about 30 minutes; don't overdo it, or they'll get too soft. Drain well.

mascarpone and citrus kugel

MAKES 10 TO 12 SERVINGS

For a holiday meal, weekend lunch, brunch, or any time that you're feeling indulgent, make this sweet, over-the-top kugel. Okay, I know it has sour cream and mascarpone *and* butter, but few Jewish cooks ever got famous for their diet cuisine. Just go for it and head to the gym the day after. And keep saying to yourself that the kids need a lot of calcium for their growing bones.

Kugel

One 12-ounce package medium egg noodles

8 tablespoons (1 stick) unsalted butter, cut into 8 pieces and softened

5 large eggs

$3/4$ cup granulated sugar

24 ounces sour cream ($2^{1}/_{2}$ cups)

8 ounces mascarpone

1 teaspoon vanilla extract

Grated zest of 1 orange

Grated zest of $1/2$ lemon

Topping

$1/2$ cup crushed cornflakes

2 tablespoons light brown sugar

1 teaspoon ground cinnamon

$1/4$ teaspoon freshly grated nutmeg

8 tablespoons (1 stick) unsalted butter, melted

1. Position a rack in the center of the oven and preheat the oven to 350°F. Lightly butter a 13 × 9-inch baking dish. To make the kugel, bring a large pot of lightly salted water to a boil over high heat. Add the noodles and cook just until tender, about 8 minutes. Drain well and return to the pot. Add the butter and stir until the butter melts and coats the noodles.

2. Whisk the eggs and sugar in a medium bowl. Add the sour cream, mascarpone, vanilla, and orange and lemon zests, and whisk just until combined. Do not over-whisk, or the mascarpone will separate. Pour over the noodles and mix to combine. Spread evenly in the baking dish.

3. To make the topping, mix the cornflakes, brown sugar, cinnamon, and nutmeg. Sprinkle evenly over the kugel and drizzle with the butter.

4. Bake until the kugel feels set when pressed in the center, about 30 minutes. Let stand 10 minutes. Cut into squares and serve warm.

mashed potato and vegetable kugel

MAKES 8 MAIN-COURSE SERVINGS, 10 TO 12 SIDE-DISH SERVINGS

Kugel is always welcome as a side dish at Shabbat and holiday dinners, but we like to serve this substantial potato dish for a main course with a fresh green salad, too. It's brightly colored with peppers, spinach, and herbs, so it will add a festive touch to any table, whether or not it's a special occasion. Leftovers disappear at lunch the next day.

4 tablespoons olive oil

$\frac{1}{4}$ cup plain dry bread crumbs

4 pounds baking potatoes, such as russet or Burbank, peeled and halved

1 medium red bell pepper, cored, seeded, and cut into $\frac{1}{4}$-inch dice

1 medium green bell pepper, cored, seeded, and cut into $\frac{1}{4}$-inch dice

1 small red onion, cut into $\frac{1}{4}$-inch dice

3 garlic cloves, chopped

$\frac{3}{4}$ cup heavy cream

12 tablespoons ($1\frac{1}{2}$ sticks) unsalted butter

3 large eggs, beaten

One 15-ounce container ricotta cheese

3 cups (12 ounces) shredded mozzarella cheese

$\frac{1}{4}$ cup chopped fresh basil, or a combination of 2 tablespoons chopped fresh basil and 1 tablespoon each chopped fresh thyme and rosemary

$1\frac{1}{2}$ teaspoons kosher salt

$\frac{1}{2}$ teaspoon freshly ground black pepper

1. Position a rack in the center of the oven and preheat the oven to 350°F. Generously brush the inside of a 10-inch springform pan with 2 tablespoons of oil. Coat the inside of the pan with 2 tablespoons of bread crumbs.

2. Place the potatoes in a large saucepan and add enough salted water to cover the potatoes by 1 inch. Bring to a boil over high heat. Reduce the heat to medium and cook until the potatoes are tender, about 25 minutes. Drain well. Let the potatoes stand uncovered for 10 minutes.

3. Meanwhile, heat the remaining 2 tablespoons of oil in a large skillet over medium heat. Add the red and green bell peppers, onion, and garlic. Cook, stirring often, until the vegetables are softened, about 8 minutes. Cool the vegetables completely.

4. Bring the heavy cream and 8 tablespoons (1 stick) of butter to a simmer in a small saucepan over medium heat. Transfer the potatoes to the bowl of a standing electric mixer fitted with the paddle blade. On low speed, beat the potatoes, gradually adding the warm cream mixture. Continue beating, occasionally scraping down the sides of the bowl, until the potatoes are smooth. Beat on medium-low speed for 1 minute to be sure the potatoes are smooth. Return the speed to low, and beat in the cooled vegetables, eggs, ricotta, mozzarella, basil, salt, and pepper.

5. Spread the potato mixture evenly in the springform pan. Melt the remaining 4 tablespoons of butter in a small saucepan over low heat (or use the microwave oven). Sprinkle the potato casserole with the remaining 2 tablespoons of bread crumbs, and drizzle with the melted butter. Bake until the casserole feels somewhat firm when pressed in the center, about 1 hour.

6. Transfer the casserole to a wire cake rack. Cool for 20 minutes. Remove the sides of the pan and cut the kugel into wedges. Serve warm. (The kugel can also be cooled and served at room temperature, or it can be made up to 1 day ahead, cooled, covered with plastic wrap, and refrigerated. If you want to reheat it, cover it with aluminum foil and bake in a preheated 300°F oven until heated through, about 30 minutes.)

spanish smashed potatoes
with fried eggs

MAKES 6 SERVINGS

Spanish cooks have learned the trick of cooking their potatoes in herbed water, all the better to infuse flavor into the spuds. Once that's done, they are fried up with onions and garlic, topped with cilantro and salsa, and finished off with a fried egg. This spicy and surprisingly filling dish is equally good for dinner and brunch.

1½ pounds red- or white-skinned boiling potatoes, scrubbed but unpeeled

½ teaspoon dried thyme

3 bay leaves

Kosher salt

6 tablespoons olive oil, plus more as needed

1 medium onion, thinly sliced

3 garlic cloves, chopped

¾ teaspoon dried oregano

Freshly ground black pepper to taste

6 large eggs

3 tablespoons chopped fresh cilantro

1 lime, cut into wedges

Tomato-Cilantro Salsa (page 162), or use store-bought salsa

1. Place the potatoes, thyme, and bay leaves in a medium saucepan and add enough lightly salted cold water to barely cover the potatoes. Bring to a boil over high heat. Reduce the heat to medium-low and simmer the potatoes until they are tender when pierced with the tip of a knife, about 20 minutes. Drain and discard the bay leaves. Using a potato masher, coarsely smash the unpeeled potatoes.

2. Heat 3 tablespoons of oil in a large heavy skillet, preferably cast iron, over medium heat. Add the onion and cook until it is translucent, about 5 minutes. Add the garlic and oregano and stir until the garlic is fragrant, about 1 minute. Add the smashed potatoes and cook, turning occasionally with a spatula, until the potatoes are lightly browned, about 10 minutes. Season the potatoes with salt and pepper.

3. When the potatoes are almost done, heat the remaining 3 tablespoons oil in another large skillet over medium-high heat. Crack 3 eggs into the skillet and fry them according to your preference—I like sunny-side up for this dish. In that case, fry the eggs just until the whites are set, about 1 minute. Season the eggs with salt and pepper. Transfer to the skillet of potatoes. Repeat with the remaining 3 eggs. Sprinkle with the cilantro.

4. Serve the potatoes and eggs from the skillet, with the lime wedges and salsa passed on the side for seasoning.

zucchini and tomato frittata

MAKES 4 TO 6 SERVINGS

You can put just about anything in a frittata, and it'll always be good. This one is loaded with mozzarella cheese and basil. Baking gives the frittata a very light, fluffy texture, which is just the way I like it. Like so many of the recipes in this chapter, this dish is excellent as a family supper, lunch, or brunch.

2 tablespoons olive oil

1 tablespoon unsalted butter

1 large zucchini, cut into $1/2$-inch dice

1 small red onion, halved lengthwise and thinly sliced into half-moons

$1/4$ cup drained and chopped ($1/4$-inch dice) sun-dried tomatoes or 1 ripe plum tomato, cut into $1/2$-inch dice

10 large eggs

1 teaspoon kosher salt

$1/2$ teaspoon freshly ground black pepper

3 cups (12 ounces) shredded mozzarella cheese

$3/4$ cup packed fresh basil, coarsely chopped

1. Position a rack in the center of the oven and preheat to 350°F. Heat the oil and butter in a 10-inch nonstick ovenproof skillet over medium heat. Add the zucchini, onion, and sun-dried tomatoes. Cook, stirring often, until the zucchini is tender, about 10 minutes.

2. Meanwhile, whisk the eggs, salt, and pepper until the eggs are uniformly bright yellow. Stir in $1^1/2$ cups of mozzarella and the basil. Pour into the skillet and stir to combine the vegetables and eggs.

3. Carefully transfer the skillet to the oven and bake until the eggs are fluffy and golden brown, 15 to 20 minutes. Sprinkle with the remaining cheese and bake until the cheese melts, about 3 minutes.

4. Slide the frittata onto a platter. Serve hot or cooled to room temperature, cut into wedges.

tuscan
vegetable soup
(recipe page 25)

chilled sweet pepper
and pineapple soup

(recipe page 31)

arugula, fennel,
and orange salad

(recipe page 50)

asparagus and tofu salad
with soy-wasabi vinaigrette
(recipe page 48)

grilled chicken on mixed greens
with mango salsa (recipe page 74)

OPPOSITE:
chicken and mushroom
fricassee (recipe page 75)

korean-style short ribs
(recipe page 108)

grilled skirt steak with roasted
vegetable salsa (recipe page 98)

OPPOSITE:

**tarragon salmon fillets
with vegetable ragout**

(recipe page 118)

**cornflake-crusted sea bass
with corn and black bean salsa**

(recipe page 126)

**tuna-basil burgers
with aioli and arugula**

(recipe page 140)

OPPOSITE:
**sicilian-style
stuffed bell peppers**
(recipe page 152)

**grilled vegetables escabeche
with citrus vinaigrette**
(recipe page 164)

**spanish smashed potatoes
with fried eggs**
(recipe page 158)

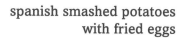

capellini with anchovies
and toasted bread crumbs

(recipe page 172)

orecchiette with
broccoli rabe and sausages

(recipe page 186)

OPPOSITE:
provençale potato latkes with
roasted red pepper relish

(recipe page 148)

OPPOSITE:

**four-cheese baked ziti
with herbed crumbs**

(recipe page 190)

**strawberries and marsala
with honeyed cream**

(recipe page 234)

**sweet grilled cheese sandwich
with mascarpone and orange**

(recipe page 217)

poached apricots
with lemon and thyme
(recipe page 213)

spiedini romano

MAKES 4 SANDWICHES

This golden brown, egg-dipped cheese sandwich is usually served as an appetizer at Italian restaurants. In our house, we call it Italian French Dip, happily eating it for lunch or a simple supper. We are anchovy and garlic lovers, and sometimes I think that Ali is going to grab a spoon to drink the sauce from the bowl. If you prefer, serve the spiedini with a wedge of lemon instead of the sauce, but you won't know what you're missing!

½ **recipe Anchovy-Garlic Sauce (page 172)**

8 **slices firm white sandwich bread**

12 **slices mozzarella cheese, trimmed to fit the bread**

½ **cup all-purpose flour**

½ **teaspoon kosher salt**

¼ **teaspoon freshly ground black pepper**

3 **large eggs, beaten**

½ **cup olive oil**

1. Make the anchovy-garlic sauce and let it stand while making the sandwiches.

2. Position a rack in the center of the oven and preheat the oven to 250°F. Line a baking sheet with paper towels.

3. Make 4 sandwiches, using 2 pieces of bread and 3 slices of mozzarella for each. Place the flour, salt, and pepper in a wide, shallow bowl. Beat the eggs in another, similar bowl. Working in two batches, coat two sandwiches with the flour, then dip in the eggs, letting the excess egg drip off.

4. Heat the oil over high heat until very hot but not smoking. Place the sandwiches in the hot oil and cook, turning once, until both sides are golden, about 4 minutes. Transfer to the baking sheet and keep warm while frying the second batch.

5. Cut each sandwich in half diagonally. Serve hot, with small bowls of the sauce for dipping.

havarti quesadillas with arugula and tomato-cilantro salsa

MAKES 4 TO 6 SERVINGS

Quesadillas alone can be a satisfying light meal, but pair them with a more substantial soup or salad (such as the Mexican Chopped Salad on page 60), and everyone's appetite will be satisfied. Havarti is one of the few cheeses that is relatively easy to find in a meat-free version made with vegetable rennet, so I use it a lot in my cooking. It melts beautifully, and its mild flavor is offset by the peppery arugula. Another time, substitute the Corn and Black Bean Salsa on page 126 for the Tomato-Cilantro version here.

Tomato-Cilantro Salsa

3 ripe plum tomatoes, cut into ¼-inch dice

1 small red onion, chopped

½ cup chopped fresh cilantro

1 jalapeño, seeded and minced

1½ tablespoons fresh lime juice

1 tablespoon extra-virgin olive oil

Kosher salt and freshly ground black pepper to taste

5 cups (about 1¼ pounds) shredded Havarti cheese

Ten 8- to 10-inch flour tortillas

1 cup (about 4 ounces) packed coarsely chopped arugula

1. To make the salsa, mix the tomatoes, onion, cilantro, jalapeño, lime juice, and oil in a medium bowl. Season with salt and pepper. Let stand at room temperature while making the quesadillas.

2. For each quesadilla, sprinkle ¾ cup of Havarti on a tortilla, leaving a ½-inch border around the edges. Scatter with about 3 tablespoons of the arugula and ¼ cup of the salsa. Sprinkle with ¼ cup more Havarti. Top with another tortilla and press firmly.

3. Position a rack in the center of the oven and preheat the oven to 200°F. Heat a large skillet (2 skillets will speed up the cooking) over medium-high heat. Place a quesadilla in the skillet and cook until the underside is browned, about 2 minutes. Turn and brown the other side. Transfer to a baking sheet and keep warm in the oven while toasting the remaining quesadillas.

4. Cut each quesadilla into 6 wedges and serve hot.

grilled vegetables escabeche with citrus vinaigrette

MAKES 6 SERVINGS

When you say marinade, most people think of grilled meats, poultry, and occasionally fish. Well, let me tell you that marinated vegetables are outrageously delicious. The last time I made this, in a double batch for a family backyard cookout, we ate most of it straight from the grill, then we mixed the leftovers into pasta with some chunks of grilled chicken.

Citrus Vinaigrette

½ cup fresh orange juice

¼ cup fresh lime juice

2 tablespoon red wine vinegar

2 teaspoons sugar

½ cup olive oil

1 medium red onion, halved lengthwise and thinly sliced into half-moons

2 tablespoons chopped fresh parsley

6 garlic cloves, chopped

1 teaspoon seeded and minced jalapeño

Kosher salt and freshly ground black pepper to taste

¾ cup olive oil

1 tablespoon dried oregano

1 tablespoon dried basil

½ teaspoon hot red pepper flakes

1 large zucchini, cut on a slight diagonal into ½-inch-thick slices

1 large yellow squash, cut on a slight diagonal into ½-inch-thick slices

1 medium eggplant, preferably white eggplant, halved lengthwise, and cut into ½-inch-thick slices

2 large portobello mushrooms, stems removed

1 red bell pepper, cored, seeded, and cut into 8 wedges, seeds and ribs discarded

1 yellow bell pepper, cored, seeded, and cut into 8 wedges, seeds and ribs discarded

Toasted crusty sliced bread, for serving, optional

1. To make the vinaigrette, whisk the orange and lime juices, vinegar, and sugar in a medium bowl. Gradually whisk in the oil. Add the red onion, parsley, garlic, and jalapeño. Season with salt and pepper. Cover and set aside at room temperature while grilling the vegetables.

2. Meanwhile, mix the oil, oregano, basil, and red pepper flakes in a large bowl. Add the zucchini, yellow squash, eggplant, mushrooms, red pepper, and yellow pepper and mix to combine. Let stand at room temperature while the grill is heating, at least 15 and up to 30 minutes.

3. Build a charcoal fire in an outdoor grill and let burn until the coals are covered with white ash. (For a gas grill, preheat on high.)

4. Remove the vegetables from the marinade, shaking off and discarding excess marinade, and place on the grill. Cook, turning occasionally, until the vegetables are crisp-tender. Most of them will take about 10 minutes; just transfer them to a large platter when they're done to your liking.

5. Pour the vinaigrette over the vegetables and serve hot, cooled to room temperature, or chilled. If you wish, serve individual portions of the vegetables and the marinade on toasted bread.

roasted portobellos and vegetables with scallion oil

MAKES 4 SERVINGS

Portobello mushrooms take on a meaty texture when roasted, making this combination of vegetables more substantial than if they were left out. I purposely don't roast them for very long, for the mushrooms give off a dark liquid that will keep the dish from looking its best. You can make the scallion oil up to a week ahead.

Scallion Oil

8 scallions, whole, with ends trimmed

½ cup extra-virgin olive oil

⅛ teaspoon kosher salt

¼ cup extra-virgin olive oil, plus more for oiling pan

¼ cup chopped fresh basil, or 1 tablespoon each chopped fresh basil, rosemary, thyme, and parsley

6 large portobello mushrooms, stems removed

2 medium zucchini, each halved lengthwise

2 medium yellow squash, each halved lengthwise

4 red bell peppers, cored, seeded, and each cut into quarters

Kosher salt and freshly ground black pepper to taste

Lemon wedges, for serving

1. To make the scallion oil, bring a medium saucepan of lightly salted water to a boil over high heat. Add the scallions and cook until the tops turn a brighter shade of green, about 2 minutes. Drain and rinse well under cold running water. Squeeze well to remove the excess water from the scallions. Chop the scallions into thirds, and place in a blender. Add the ½ cup oil and salt and blend until smooth. Strain through a fine wire sieve and discard the pulp. (The scallion oil can be stored in the refrigerator in a covered container for up to 1 week. It will solidify when chilled. To serve, place the container in a bowl of warm water and let stand until the oil is liquid again.)

2. Position a rack in the top third of the oven and preheat thoroughly to 450°F. Lightly oil a large baking sheet (an 18 × 12-inch half-sheet pan works best).

3. Meanwhile, mix the ¼ cup oil and 3 tablespoons of the basil or mixed herbs in a glass measuring cup. Place the mushrooms, zucchini, yellow squash, and red peppers in a large bowl. Coat the vegetables with the herbed oil. Let stand at room temperature while the oven heats, at least 20 minutes.

4. Spread the vegetables on the baking sheet. Roast until the zucchini and yellow squash are tender, about 20 minutes. Return the zucchini and squash to the bowl. Continue roasting the mushrooms and peppers until they are tender, about 10 minutes more. The vegetables will be tender, but shouldn't take on much of a roasted color.

5. Drizzle the vegetables with a few tablespoons of the scallion oil, to taste. Sprinkle with the remaining 1 tablespoon of basil or mixed herbs and season with the salt and pepper. Serve immediately, with the lemon wedges, allowing each diner to squeeze lemon juice over the vegetables to taste.

italian vegetable stew

MAKES 6 TO 8 SERVINGS

There are times at our house when the refrigerator seems to be bursting with leftover vegetables—a few mushrooms from a pasta sauce, half a bulb of fennel from a salad . . . you know the drill. I don't mind at all. I just roll up my sleeves and make this stew. The beauty of it is how the individual vegetables harmonize into a flavorful symphony. It's even better the next day. Get out the crusty bread for sopping.

¼ cup extra-virgin olive oil

1 medium onion, coarsely chopped

3 medium carrots, cut into ¼-inch dice

6 garlic cloves, finely chopped

1 large sweet red bell pepper, cored, seeded, and cut into ½-inch dice, or 1½ cups mixed red, yellow, and green bell peppers

1 medium portobello mushroom, stem removed, cut into ½-inch dice

1 medium zucchini, cut into ½-inch dice

¼ fennel bulb, cut into ½-inch dice (about ½ cup)

1 jalapeño, seeds and ribs removed, finely chopped

1 teaspoon dried oregano

1 teaspoon dried thyme

One 14½-ounce can diced tomatoes in juice

1 large red-skinned potato, parboiled (see Note)

2 tablespoons mixed fresh herbs, such as basil and oregano

Kosher salt and freshly ground black pepper to taste

1. Heat the oil in a large saucepan over medium heat. Add the onion, carrots, and garlic and cook, stirring often, until the onions are translucent, about 6 minutes.

2. Stir in the red pepper, mushroom, zucchini, fennel, jalapeño, oregano, and thyme. Cook, stirring often, until the peppers soften, about 12 minutes.

3. Add the tomatoes with their juice, the parboiled potato, and the herbs. Cook until the tomato juices thicken and the potato is tender, about 10 minutes. Season with salt and a generous amount of pepper. Serve hot.

NOTE Acids inhibit the cooking of potatoes, so it is best to parboil potatoes before adding them to stews that include tomatoes. Boil the potato in lightly salted water for about 15 minutes, until it is beginning to yield to pressure but not tender, then drain. Or pierce the potato in a few places with a fork, and microwave on high for 5 minutes. In either case, cool the potato for a few minutes before cutting into cubes.

pasta

When I want to make a family meal that everyone will like, one that is filling and easy to prepare, the same answer comes up again and again: pasta.

I recently lost quite a few pounds on a reduced-carbohydrate diet. I also know that there are few foods more satisfying than a bowl of great-tasting pasta. I have not given it up completely and I never will, I just eat less. There's something to the Italian idea of serving pasta in small portions. Even in this book, I use the accepted American yield of four to six servings per pound of dried pasta. But I want to encourage you to serve four portions of approximately three ounces each for supper, and to save the remaining for the next day's lunch. Often, with the addition of vinegar and oil, last night's supper can become today's pasta salad. Fusilli with Red Peppers, Goat Cheese, and Basil on page 176 and Fettuccine with Wild Mushrooms, Fra Diavolo on page 181 lend themselves perfectly to this concept.

My kids love plain old spaghetti with tomato sauce and macaroni and cheese as much as anyone's. But they have also developed a strong preference for Penne with Roasted Lamb Sauce (page 182) and Four-Cheese Baked Ziti with Herbed Crumbs (page 190). They joke that their friends think that ravioli only comes out of a can and that macaroni and cheese out of a box. I don't expect people to simmer tomato sauce for two hours on a weeknight—even I use a jar of marinara sauce in my ziti. But I would like to see you think ahead and make a big batch of sauce when you do have the time and freeze the results, because nothing beats homemade pasta sauce.

capellini with anchovies and toasted bread crumbs

MAKES 4 TO 6 SERVINGS

We like anchovies and garlic in our house—yes, even the kids. So when we want a pasta dish that isn't too heavy, a meal that needs only a green salad to round things out, we often turn to this dish, loaded with the flavors of southern Italy. Also, it includes two components that I use in other recipes, Toasted Bread Crumbs (with the escarole on page 198) and Anchovy-Garlic Sauce (with Spiedini Romano sandwiches on page 161).

Toasted Bread Crumbs

2 tablespoons unsalted butter

2 tablespoons olive oil

1 cup panko (crisp Japanese bread crumbs)

½ cup chopped fresh parsley

Kosher salt and freshly ground black pepper to taste

Anchovy-Garlic Sauce

6 tablespoons unsalted butter

2 tablespoons olive oil

12 garlic cloves, chopped

6 anchovy fillets, drained and chopped

1 tablespoon dried oregano

½ cup fresh lemon juice

2½ cups Vegetable Broth (page 44) or vegetable bouillon

1 tablespoon chopped fresh parsley

Kosher salt and freshly ground black pepper to taste

1 pound capellini (angel-hair pasta)

Freshly grated Parmesan cheese, for serving

1. To make the bread crumbs, melt the butter with the oil in a large skillet over medium heat. Add the bread crumbs and cook, stirring often, until the crumbs are golden brown, about 4 minutes. Remove from the heat and stir in the parsley. Season with salt and pepper. Set aside.

2. Bring a large pot of lightly salted water to a boil over high heat. Meanwhile, make the sauce: Melt 2 tablespoons of butter with the oil in a large skillet. Add the garlic, anchovies, and oregano. Cook, whisking often, until the garlic is lightly browned and the anchovies are dissolved, about 1 minute. Add the broth and lemon juice. Bring to a simmer over high heat. Reduce the heat to medium and simmer to blend the flavors, about 10 minutes. Remove the sauce from the heat and cover to keep warm.

3. Add the pasta to the water and cook until al dente, about 4 minutes. Drain well. Return the pasta to the cooking pot.

4. Off the heat, whisk the remaining 4 tablespoons butter into the sauce. Add the parsley. Season with salt and pepper. Stir into the pasta. Serve immediately, topping each serving with a generous mound of the toasted bread crumbs. Pass the Parmesan on the side.

capellini with smoked salmon and lemon cream

MAKES 2 TO 4 SERVINGS

This creamy pasta is definitely on the rich side and is perhaps best appreciated in small portions, but that is part of its charm. Both the pasta and the sauce cook quickly, so look over the recipe before you begin cooking to get a handle on the timing, as both components should be done about the same time.

3 tablespoons extra-virgin olive oil

1 small onion, finely chopped

3 garlic cloves, finely chopped

½ pound sliced smoked salmon, cut into ½-inch pieces

1½ cups heavy cream

½ cup fresh lemon juice

2 tablespoons unsalted butter

½ teaspoon Worcestershire sauce

1 teaspoon hot red pepper sauce

3 scallions, white and green parts, thinly sliced

¼ cup coarsely chopped basil

Zest of 1 lemon

½ pound capellini (half of a 1-pound box)

Sea salt and freshly ground black pepper to taste

1. Bring a large pot of lightly salted water to a boil over high heat.

2. Meanwhile, heat the oil in a large saucepan over medium heat. Add the onion and garlic and cook, stirring often, until the onion is translucent, about 5 minutes. Add the salmon and cook for 1 minute. Add the heavy cream and lemon juice and bring to a boil. Reduce the heat to low and simmer until lightly thickened, 2 to 3 minutes. Stir in the butter, Worcestershire, and hot red pepper sauce. Stir in the scallions, basil, and lemon zest. Set the sauce aside.

3. Meanwhile, about 4 minutes before the sauce is done, add the pasta to the water and stir well. Cook, stirring often to discourage the pasta from sticking, until the pasta is al dente, about 4 minutes. Scoop out and reserve ½ cup of the cooking water. Drain the pasta well and return it to the pot.

4. Add the sauce to the pasta and toss, adding enough of the pasta water to thin the sauce as desired. Season with salt and pepper. Serve hot.

fusilli with red peppers, goat cheese, and basil

MAKES 4 TO 6 SERVINGS

This pasta features many of the most easily identifiable flavors of Mediterranean cuisine—tangy kalamata olives, sharp and creamy goat cheese, bold garlic, and perfumed basil. Once the pasta is cooked, supper will be on the table in just a few minutes. If cooked slowly, the garlic shouldn't be overwhelming, but reduce the amount if you wish. Be sure to purchase pitted kalamata olives packed in vinegary brine, as the brine will be used in the pasta.

½ cup extra-virgin olive oil

15 garlic cloves, thinly sliced

½ teaspoon hot red pepper flakes

2 medium red bell peppers, cored, seeded, and cut into thin matchsticks

1 medium red onion, quartered lengthwise, then cut crosswise into thin slices

1 pound fusilli, or other twisted pasta

1 cup pitted and coarsely chopped kalamata olives

1 cup coarsely chopped fresh basil

¼ cup vinegar brine drained from the kalamata olives

2 tablespoons unsalted butter

¼ pound rindless goat cheese, crumbled

Kosher salt and freshly ground black pepper to taste

1. Bring a large pot of lightly salted water to a boil over high heat.

2. Meanwhile, combine ¼ cup of oil with the garlic and red pepper flakes in a large skillet. Cook over low heat until the garlic is golden brown, about 10 minutes. Add the bell peppers and onion and cook, stirring often, until the vegetables wilt, about 10 minutes longer. Remove from the heat and cover to keep warm.

3. Add the fusilli to the boiling water and cook until al dente, about 8 minutes. Scoop out and reserve ½ cup of the cooking water. Drain the pasta and return it to the cooking pot.

4. Add the reserved vegetables, remaining ¼ cup oil, olives, basil, olive vinegar brine, and butter to the pasta. Mix, adding enough of the reserved pasta water to make a light sauce. Add the goat cheese and mix again. Season with salt and pepper. Serve hot.

Garlic

Dog is man's best friend, but garlic is the chef's best friend. At least it's this chef's best friend.

Some people find garlic too strong. I argue that they find the flavor of *burned* garlic too strong.

In the interest of fast cooking, garlic is often sautéed in hot oil, which may cook it quickly, but gives it an acrid taste. I cook my garlic slowly, gently allowing it to turn from ivory white to golden brown. Cooked this way, the flavor of garlic may be a revelation to you.

On the other hand, I know that I like a lot of garlic, and anytime that you want to reduce the amount called for in a recipe, go right ahead.

sun-dried tomato and cheese kreplach with pesto

MAKES 6 SERVINGS

Stuffing kreplach at home is less daunting when you have kids in the house to help out. In fact, it's a fun project for the whole family. This bright-tasting filling has sun-dried tomatoes, two kinds of cheese, roasted garlic, and herbs, pulled together with a pesto sauce. Wonton wrappers stand in for dough made from scratch.

Kreplach

$1/2$ cups (6 ounces) shredded mozzarella

1 cup ricotta cheese

5 roasted garlic cloves (see page 203), or use store-bought roasted garlic

$1/4$ cup drained and diced ($1/4$-inch) sun-dried tomatoes

2 tablespoons chopped fresh basil

1 tablespoon chopped fresh oregano

2 tablespoons extra-virgin olive oil

Kosher salt and freshly ground black pepper to taste

One 12-ounce package 3-inch square wonton wrappers

$1/4$ cup Pesto (recipe follows)

2 tablespoons unsalted butter

Freshly grated Parmesan cheese, for serving

1. To make the filling, chill the bowl of a food processor in the freezer for 10 minutes. Attach to the processor, and add the mozzarella, ricotta, roasted garlic, sun-dried tomatoes, basil, and oregano. Process until smooth, scraping down the bowl as needed. With the machine running, add the oil. Season with salt and pepper.

2. Lightly flour a baking sheet. Place a wonton wrapper in front of you. Spoon a teaspoon of the filling onto the center of the wrapper. Dip your finger in water and moisten the edges of the wrapper. Fold the wrapper in half, point to point, to enclose the filling and create a stuffed triangle. Repeat with all of the wrappers and the filling. (The kreplach can be prepared up to 4 hours ahead, covered with plastic wrap and refrigerated.)

3. Bring a large pot of lightly salted water to a boil over high heat. A few at a time (to keep the water boiling), add all of the kreplach to the water. Cook until they float to the top of the water, about 3 minutes. Because the wonton skins are delicate, it is best not to drain the kreplach in a colander. Instead, use a large wire skimmer or slotted spoon to transfer the kreplach to a large bowl. Scoop out and reserve ½ cup of the pasta cooking water.

4. Add the pesto and butter to the bowl. Mix gently, adding enough of the reserved pasta water to loosen the pasta and create a light sauce. Serve, with the cheese passed on the side.

Condiment Heaven

In my refrigerators, at home and in my various professional kitchens, you'll find jars of different condiments, including the Yemenite zhug (page 132), basil pesto (page 180), and Black Olive Pesto (page 189) from this book. The zhug and basil pesto are great for bringing another level of aromatic flavor to soups or stews—just stir in a spoonful or two to taste. Either of the three can be mixed with mayonnaise for a quick dip for vegetables or fried or grilled foods. The pestos can even be used as sandwich spreads. They're all simple to make and keep for a few weeks, and they will add simple variety to your meals.

RECIPE CONTINUES

Pesto

MAKES 2 CUPS

You can find kosher pesto at the market, either dairy (with Parmesan cheese) or pareve (without cheese), but I prefer to make my own from my bountiful summer crop of basil for a fraction of the price. Lacking homegrown basil, one large bunch from a farmer's market will provide enough leaves for this recipe. The addition of parsley to the basil boosts the amount of chlorophyll, and helps keep the pesto nice and green. While pine nuts are the classic nut for many pesto recipes, other nuts, such as almonds or walnuts, also have their fans. Frankly, the nuts are used more for emulsifying the pesto than for flavor. In this recipe, I grind the nuts right into the pesto in the traditional manner, but I often stir the slivered almonds into the finished pesto for extra crunch. Filmed over with a little olive oil and refrigerated, the pesto will last for a few weeks, or as long as it takes for you to use it all, which usually isn't very long.

8 garlic cloves, crushed under a knife and peeled

2 cups packed basil leaves

1/2 cup packed parsley leaves

1/4 cup slivered almonds, toasted (see Note)

1 cup extra-virgin olive oil, plus more for storage

Kosher salt and freshly ground black pepper to taste

1. Fit a food processor with the metal chopping blade. With the machine running, drop the garlic through the feed tube to mince the garlic. Turn off the food processor.

2. Add the basil, parsley, and almonds to the food processor. With the machine running, slowly pour the oil through the feed tube. Process until smooth, scraping down the sides of the bowl as needed. Season with salt and pepper.

3. To store the pesto, transfer it to a covered container and smooth the top. Pour a thin layer of oil over the top. Refrigerate for up to 4 weeks. After using the pesto, smooth any remaining pesto in the container and add more oil to the container.

NOTE To toast the almonds, spread them on a baking sheet. (The tray of a toaster oven is fine for this.) Bake in a preheated 350°F oven (or toaster oven), stirring occasionally, until the almonds are lightly browned, about 10 minutes. Cool.

DAIRY VARIATION

Stir 1/2 cup freshly grated Parmesan cheese into the finished pesto.

fettuccine with wild mushrooms, fra diavolo

MAKES 4 TO 6 SERVINGS

A few tricks will make this dish as good as it can be. Cook the mushrooms over low heat so they slowly release their juices, then increase the heat to reduce and intensify the liquid. Use a few chopped tomatoes to highlight the fresh mushroom flavor; tomato sauce is too heavy. And finish with a drizzle of fruity, flavorful olive oil.

$\frac{1}{3}$ cup plus $\frac{1}{4}$ cup extra-virgin olive oil, plus more for serving

12 garlic cloves, thinly sliced

$\frac{3}{4}$ teaspoon hot red pepper flakes

1 pound assorted wild mushrooms (cremini, chanterelles, stemmed shiitake), sliced

Kosher salt and freshly ground black pepper to taste

5 ripe plum tomatoes, cut into 1-inch dice

1 pound fettuccine

$\frac{1}{3}$ cup coarsely chopped basil

1. Combine $\frac{1}{3}$ cup of oil, the garlic, and the red pepper flakes in a large skillet over low heat. Cook, stirring occasionally, until the garlic is light golden brown, about 15 minutes.

2. Add the mushrooms and season with salt and pepper. Continue cooking on low heat, stirring occasionally, until the mushrooms release their liquid, about 10 minutes. Add the tomatoes and increase the heat to medium-high. Cook, stirring often, until the mushroom liquid evaporates and the tomatoes begin to break down, about 6 minutes. Remove from the heat and cover to keep the sauce warm.

3. Meanwhile, bring a large pot of lightly salted water to a boil over high heat. Add the fettuccine and cook until the pasta is al dente, about 8 minutes. Reserve $\frac{1}{2}$ cup of the pasta cooking water. Drain the pasta well and return it to the cooking pot.

4. Return the sauce to a simmer. Stir in the basil, reserved pasta water, and remaining $\frac{1}{4}$ cup of oil and cook for 2 minutes. Stir the sauce into the pasta. Serve immediately with olive oil on the side for drizzling onto each serving.

DAIRY VARIATION

Serve with Parmesan cheese.

penne with roasted lamb sauce

MAKES 2 QUARTS SAUCE, ENOUGH FOR 2 POUNDS PASTA

This beautifully spiced sauce is fragrant with cinnamon, chunky with lamb, and roasted to concentrate the flavors. You will love it, especially when you find the spare quart in your freezer.

2 pounds lamb stew meat, cut into 1-inch chunks

One 28-ounce can crushed tomatoes

2 medium onions, halved lengthwise and thinly sliced into half-moons

1½ cups water

1 cup dry white wine, such as Chardonnay

6 garlic cloves, chopped

Two 3-inch cinnamon sticks

1 teaspoon dried oregano

1 teaspoon kosher salt, plus more to taste

1 teaspoon freshly ground black pepper, plus more to taste

1 pound dried penne

1. Position a rack in the center of the oven and preheat the oven to 350°F. Lightly oil the inside of a small roasting pan, about 15 × 10 inches.

2. Combine the lamb, tomatoes, onions, water, wine, garlic, cinnamon sticks, oregano, salt, and pepper in the roasting pan. Cover tightly. Bake until the lamb is fork tender, about 2 hours, 15 minutes.

3. Remove from the oven. Discard the cinnamon sticks. Skim any fat off the surface of the sauce. Stir well with a wooden spoon, allowing the lamb to break up into small pieces. Taste and adjust the seasoning with salt and pepper. Transfer half of the sauce to a covered container, cool completely, and freeze for another meal. (The sauce can be frozen for up to 3 months.)

4. Meanwhile, bring a large pot of lightly salted water to a boil over high heat. Add the penne and cook until al dente, about 9 minutes. Drain the pasta well and return it to the pot.

5. Add the remaining sauce to the pasta and stir well. Serve hot.

egg noodles with zucchini and lemon sauce

MAKES 4 TO 6 SERVINGS

This light and delicate pasta is great for a summer supper. You'll need a V-slicer to cut the zucchini into thin shreds. This useful utensil, an inexpensive version of a mandoline (the pricey professional French slicing implement), can be used to slice potatoes for kugel and other chores. Or you can cut the zucchini with a knife into the thinnest possible matchsticks.

12 ounces medium egg noodles

1 cup extra-virgin olive oil

16 garlic cloves, chopped

1 teaspoon hot red pepper flakes

2 large zucchini, cut into fine julienne on a V-slicer or mandoline, or by hand

Kosher salt and freshly ground black pepper to taste

½ cup fresh lemon juice

½ cup packed basil leaves

4 tablespoons unsalted butter, at room temperature

Grated zest of 2 lemons

Freshly grated Parmesan cheese, for serving

1. Bring a large pot of lightly salted water to a boil over high heat and add the noodles. Cook until tender, about 7 minutes.

2. Time this next step so the zucchini is done at about the same time as the noodles. Combine the oil, garlic, and red pepper flakes in a large skillet over low heat. Cook, stirring occasionally, until the garlic is golden brown, about 8 minutes. Add the zucchini and season with salt and pepper. Cook just until wilted, about 2 minutes. Add the lemon juice, and ¼ cup water and bring to a simmer. Stir in the basil, butter, and lemon zest.

3. Drain the noodles and return them to the pot. Add the zucchini mixture and mix well. Serve, with the cheese passed on the side.

potato pierogi with cabbage, fennel, and caraway

MAKES 4 TO 6 SERVINGS

Are pierogi Jewish ravioli, or are ravioli Italian pierogi? Well, I can't imagine serving pierogi with tomato sauce, so this dish plays up pierogi's Eastern European connection with cabbage, fennel, caraway, and onions. An hour's cooking gives the cabbage a silky texture and a lightly caramelized sheen that enhances its plain reputation. Look for pierogi in the refrigerated section, in the delicatessen department, or in the frozen food cases.

$\frac{1}{3}$ **cup olive oil**

1 large onion, thinly sliced

1 small fennel bulb, cut in half lengthwise and cut crosswise into thin slices

One 3-pound head cabbage, cut into quarters, core removed, and cut into thin shreds

1 tablespoon dried thyme

1 teaspoon caraway seeds

$\frac{1}{4}$ **cup chopped fresh parsley**

Kosher salt and freshly ground black pepper to taste

24 potato pierogi

4 tablespoons unsalted butter

1. Heat the oil in a very large (preferably nonstick) skillet over medium-high heat. Add the onion and fennel and cook until they begin to soften, about 3 minutes. A handful at a time, add the cabbage and cook, waiting for the first batch to wilt before adding more. Stir in the thyme and caraway. Reduce the heat to medium. Cover and cook until the cabbage is tender, about 40 minutes. Uncover and cook, stirring occasionally, until the cabbage is golden and lightly caramelized, about 20 minutes more. Stir in the parsley. Season with salt and pepper. Transfer the cabbage to a large serving platter and cover with foil to keep warm.

2. Meanwhile, bring a large pot of lightly salted water to a boil over high heat. Add the pierogi and cook until tender, about 6 minutes. Gently drain in a colander, to avoid breaking the pierogi.

3. Wipe out the skillet, add the butter, and melt over medium-high heat. Add the pierogi and cook, turning with a spatula, until lightly browned, about 5 minutes. (If the skillet isn't nonstick, check to be sure that the pierogi don't stick to the pan.) Place the browned pierogies on top of the cabbage and serve.

PAREVE VARIATION

Substitute olive oil for the butter in step 3.

orecchiette with broccoli rabe and sausages

MAKES 4 SERVINGS

The faintly bitter flavor of broccoli rabe goes hand-in-hand with sausage. But that doesn't mean that you shouldn't substitute broccoli florets or the thin broccolini, if you wish. And be sure to use curved or twisty pasta (fusilli would be good) to catch the bits of vegetable in the sauce.

1 pound orechiette pasta

⅓ cup olive oil

12 garlic cloves, thinly sliced

½ teaspoon hot red pepper flakes, or more to taste

½ pound veal, turkey, or Polish sausage, cut slightly on the diagonal into ¼-inch-thick slices

1 pound broccoli rabe, well rinsed and coarsely chopped

1 teaspoon dried oregano

⅓ cup plus 1 tablespoon fresh lemon juice

Kosher salt and freshly ground black pepper to taste

1. Bring a large pot of lightly salted water to a boil over high heat. Add the pasta and cook until al dente, about 8 minutes.

2. Meanwhile, make the sauce. Combine the oil, garlic, and red pepper flakes in a large skillet. Cook over low heat, stirring often, just until the garlic begins to brown, about 3 minutes. Add the sausage and increase the heat to medium. Cook, stirring occasionally, until the sausage heats through, about 3 minutes more. Stir in the broccoli rabe and oregano. Add ½ cup water and cover partially with the lid. Cook, stirring occasionally, until the broccoli rabe is barely tender, about 5 minutes. Stir in the lemon juice and season with salt and pepper. Keep warm.

3. Drain the pasta and return it to the pot. Add the broccoli rabe and mix well. Serve hot.

PAREVE VARIATION

Omit the sausage.

DAIRY VARIATION

Omit the sausage and serve the pasta with lots of freshly grated Parmesan cheese.

rigatoni with short ribs ragú

MAKES 4 TO 6 SERVINGS

When the kids ask for a meaty tomato sauce, this is the one to make. This gutsy sauce needs sturdy pasta to stand up to it, such as the suggested rigatoni. It is well worth the small bit of extra effort to make a double batch, freezing half for another meal.

¼ cup extra-virgin olive oil

2 pounds boneless beef flanken (cross-cut short ribs), cut into 1-inch pieces

2 medium onions, chopped

7 garlic cloves, sliced

1 teaspoon dried oregano

3 tablespoons all-purpose flour

3 cups beef broth, homemade, canned, or prepared bouillon

One 28-ounce can crushed tomatoes

2 bay leaves

1 teaspoon kosher salt

1 teaspoon freshly ground black pepper

1 pound rigatoni

1. Position a rack in the center of the oven and preheat the oven to 350°F. Heat the oil in a Dutch oven over medium-high heat. Add the flanken and cook, turning the meat occasionally, until it is lightly browned on all sides, about 10 minutes. Add the onions, garlic, and oregano. Reduce the heat to medium. Cook, stirring often, until the onion is translucent, about 5 minutes. Sprinkle with the flour, stir well, and cook for 3 minutes longer. Stir in the broth, tomatoes, bay leaves, salt, and pepper. Bring to a simmer and cover tightly.

2. Place the pot in the oven and cook, stirring occasionally, until the flanken is very tender, about 1½ hours. Remove from the heat. Let stand 5 minutes and skim any fat from the surface of the sauce.

3. Meanwhile, bring a large pot of lightly salted water to a boil over high heat. Add the rigatoni and cook until al dente, about 9 minutes. Drain the pasta and return it to the pot. Add the sauce to the pasta and stir well. Serve hot.

spaghetti with black olive pesto

MAKES 4 TO 6 SERVINGS

Because we are rarely without a jar of Black Olive Pesto in the refrigerator, we can have dinner on the table in less than five minutes after draining the pasta. I like it just the way it is, but you could add a can of drained tuna for a heartier meal.

1 pound spaghetti

1 lemon

⅓ cup Black Olive Pesto (recipe follows)

2 tablespoons extra-virgin olive oil

2 tablespoons unsalted butter, at room temperature

Kosher salt and freshly ground black pepper to taste

Freshly grated Parmesan cheese, for serving

1. Bring a large pot of lightly salted water to a boil over high heat. Add the pasta and cook until al dente, about 9 minutes. Scoop out and reserve ½ cup of the cooking water. Drain the pasta and return it to the pot.

2. Grate the lemon zest into the pasta. Halve the lemon and squeeze the juice (you should have about 2 tablespoons), and add to the pasta, along with the pesto, olive oil, and butter. Toss, adding enough of the pasta water to loosen the pesto and make a light sauce. Season with salt and pepper, using a light hand with the sauce.

3. Serve hot, with the cheese passed on the side.

PAREVE VARIATION

Omit the Parmesan cheese and butter; double the oil.

Black Olive Pesto

MAKES 1½ CUPS

You'll find similar recipes in French and Italian cookbooks, where this unflinchingly flavored condiment is called *tapenade* and *olivada,* respectively. I call it Black Olive Pesto, because that's what it is. Use it for the Spaghetti with Black Olive Pesto, as a dip for raw vegetables, or to flavor bread crumbs for coatings (see Salmon Fillets with Black Olive Crust, page 124).

3 garlic cloves, crushed under a knife and peeled

1 cup pitted and coarsely chopped kalamata olives

¼ cup sun-dried tomatoes in oil, drained and coarsely chopped

1 tablespoons drained capers

2 anchovy fillets in oil, drained

½ cup extra-virgin olive oil

Freshly ground black pepper to taste

1. Fit a food processor with the metal chopping blade. With the machine running, drop the garlic through the feed tube to mince the garlic. Turn off the food processor.

2. Squeeze most of the moisture from the olives. Add to the food processor, with the sun-dried tomatoes, capers, and anchovies. With the machine running, slowly pour in the oil. Season with the pepper.

3. To store the pesto: Transfer it to a covered container and smooth the top. Pour a thin layer of oil over the top. Refrigerate for up to 4 weeks. After using the pesto, smooth any remaining pesto in the container and add more oil to cover.

four-cheese baked ziti with herbed crumbs

MAKES 8 SERVINGS

My family thinks this is the best baked ziti they've ever had, and I have to agree with them. It's got mozzarella, Havarti, ricotta, and Parmesan in the herbed-crumb topping, and they would eat it every night if I let them. If you have ovenproof crocks, bake it in individual servings.

1 pound ziti

Herbed Crumbs

1 cup Italian-seasoned dry bread crumbs

¼ cup Parmesan cheese

¼ cup chopped fresh parsley

½ teaspoon dried basil

½ teaspoon dried oregano

8 garlic cloves, minced

½ teaspoon kosher salt

¼ teaspoon freshly ground black pepper

⅓ cup extra-virgin olive oil

One 28-ounce jar store-bought marinara sauce

1 tablespoon dried oregano

1 teaspoon dried basil

½ teaspoon freshly ground black pepper

4 cups (1 pound) shredded mozzarella cheese

2 cups (8 ounces) shredded Havarti cheese

One 15-ounce container ricotta cheese

1. Position a rack in the center of the oven and preheat to 375°F. Lightly oil a 13 × 9-inch baking dish.

2. Bring a large pot of lightly salted water to a boil over high heat. Add the pasta and cook until al dente (it will cook further in the oven), about 8 minutes.

3. Meanwhile, make the herbed crumbs. Mix the bread crumbs, Parmesan, parsley, basil, oregano, garlic, salt, and pepper. Add the oil and mix with your hands until the crumbs feel like wet sand. Set aside.

4. Drain the pasta well and return it to the pot. Mix in the marinara sauce, oregano, basil, and pepper. Mix in half of the herbed crumbs, 3 cups of mozzarella, the Havarti, and the ricotta. Spread evenly in the baking dish. Mix the remaining herbed crumbs and 1 cup mozzarella. Sprinkle in a thick layer over the pasta.

5. Bake until the sauce is bubbling and the topping is golden, about 25 minutes. Let stand for a few minutes before serving hot.

side dishes

Too many cooks consider side dishes an afterthought, just as something to round out the meal. Ali and I apply the same awareness to side dishes as we do to our main courses, being sure that no bland food is ever served at our table. This is especially important if you want your kids to respect vegetables—give them something other than plain boiled carrots or cooked frozen peas, and they just might eat the side dish instead of pushing it around the plate.

We like to cook according to the seasons—with spring asparagus, summer-crop tomatoes, autumn root vegetables, and wintry brussels sprouts, to name a few of our favorites. Therefore, the side dishes often drive the menu and are rarely an afterthought to us.

When we're serving a meat and vegetable stir-fry or stew with plenty of sauce, it is appropriate to serve unadorned cooked rice or couscous along-side. The same goes when the dish is highly seasoned—often steamed carrots, broccoli, or something along simple lines would be best. The reverse is true when you have a main course that is on the plain side. In that case, something like the Curried Yellow Rice with Almonds and Currants (page 204) would add variety to the supper. Usually, I'm looking to add another layer of flavor and interest to the side dish, which means that it will get my family's attention, too. Take the Orzo and Garbanzos (page 199) as an example. There's nothing wrong with plain orzo. But with just a few more ingredients, it becomes so delicious that you will want to eat it on its own. That is the goal of a really good side dish.

asparagus, mushroom, and grape tomato ragout

MAKES 4 TO 6 SERVINGS

Here's a simple side dish with an elegant presentation that will dress up a grilled fish or chicken main course. If you have thin pencil asparagus, it won't need to be blanched first; just sauté it with the mushrooms for a minute before adding the tomatoes and basil.

1 pound asparagus

2 tablespoons olive oil

1 garlic clove, thinly sliced

⅛ teaspoon hot red pepper flakes

1 cup thinly sliced cremini or stemmed shiitake mushrooms

1 pint grape tomatoes

3 tablespoons chopped basil

Kosher salt and freshly ground black pepper to taste

1. Bring a medium saucepan of lightly salted water to a boil over high heat. Snap off the woody stems from the asparagus. Cut each spear, on a slight diagonal, into thirds. Add the asparagus and cook just until crisp-tender, about 3 minutes. Drain, rinse under cold water, and drain again.

2. Combine the oil, garlic, and red pepper in a large skillet over low heat. Cook, stirring occasionally, until the garlic turns golden, about 5 minutes. Add the mushrooms and increase the heat to medium. Cook, stirring occasionally, until the mushrooms soften, about 4 minutes. Stir in the asparagus, tomatoes, and basil. Cook until the tomatoes heat through, about 3 minutes. Season with salt and pepper and serve hot.

toasted barley pilaf

MAKES 4 TO 6 SERVINGS

The next time you need a starchy side dish, instead of reaching for the box of rice, try this fine alternative. Vegetable broth gives the pilaf a neutral flavor, but you can certainly use chicken stock, if you prefer. Buy pearled barley (polished grains with the bran removed), as whole-grain barley takes forever to cook.

1/3 **cup olive oil**

1 small red onion, halved lengthwise and thinly sliced into half-moons

6 garlic cloves, sliced

1/2 **teaspoon ground cumin**

1/4 **teaspoon hot red pepper flakes**

1/2 **pound (1 cup) pearled barley**

2 cups Vegetable Broth (page 44), or vegetable bouillon

1/2 **teaspoon kosher salt**

1/4 **teaspoon freshly ground black pepper**

2 tablespoons chopped fresh parsley

1. Heat the oil in a medium saucepan over low heat. Add the onion, garlic, cumin, and red pepper flakes. Cook, stirring often, until the onion is translucent, about 10 minutes.

2. Meanwhile, spread the barley in a dry medium skillet. Cook over medium heat, stirring often, until the barley is toasted. Add to the vegetables in the saucepan. Stir in the broth, salt, and pepper. Bring to a boil over high heat. Reduce the heat to medium-low and cover. Cook until the barley is just tender and has absorbed the liquid, about 45 minutes.

3. Remove from the heat and uncover. Let stand for 3 minutes. Fluff the barley with a fork and stir in the parsley. Serve hot.

shaved brussels sprouts with onions and garlic

MAKES 4 TO 6 SERVINGS

Too many cooks boil brussels sprouts to death, and then wonder why kids turn up their noses. But cut into thin slices and sautéed just until tender, they can be a revelation. Be sure to cook the sliced sprouts until their juices evaporate and form a film (called a fond) on the bottom of the skillet, as it will add a lot of flavor to the dish.

$1/3$ **cup extra-virgin olive oil**

1 large onion, chopped

6 garlic cloves, finely chopped

Two 10-ounce containers brussels sprouts, root ends trimmed

2 teaspoons sweet paprika

$1/4$ **cup water**

Grated zest of 1 lemon

2 tablespoons fresh lemon juice

1. Heat the oil in a large skillet over medium heat. Add the onion and cook, stirring often, until the onion is lightly browned, about 8 minutes. Add the garlic and cook until it gives off its aroma, about 1 minute.

2. Meanwhile, fit a food processor with the metal slicing blade. With the machine running, drop the sprouts through the feed tube to slice them very thinly. (By hand, cut the sprouts crosswise with a large, sharp knife.) Add the sprouts and paprika to the skillet and mix well. Reduce the heat to low and cover. Cook, stirring occasionally, until a thin, golden crust forms on the bottom of the skillet, 10 to 12 minutes. Add the water and cook until it evaporates, about 2 minutes.

3. Remove from the heat and stir in the lemon juice and zest. Season with salt and pepper. Serve hot.

orange-glazed baby carrots with tarragon

MAKES 4 TO 6 SERVINGS

These brightly seasoned carrots have plenty of flavor on their own, so serve them with simply prepared roasts. They're only worth making with fresh tarragon—dried just won't do—though fresh thyme or basil is a nice substitute for the tarragon. The sauce should have a balance of sweet and sour, so you may have to adjust the honey and vinegar to suit your taste.

1 pound baby-cut carrots

Grated zest from 1 juice orange

1 cup fresh orange juice

1 teaspoon apple cider vinegar

2 tablespoons honey

¼ teaspoon ground fennel seed, optional

2 tablespoons chopped fresh tarragon

Kosher salt and freshly ground black pepper to taste

1. Place the baby carrots and water to barely cover them in a small saucepan. Bring to a boil over medium heat and cover. Cook until the carrots are crisp-tender, about 6 minutes. Drain.

2. Return the carrots to the saucepan. Add the orange zest, orange juice, vinegar, honey, and fennel seed, if using. Bring to a boil over medium-high heat. Cook, uncovered, until the carrots are tender and the juice has reduced to a glaze, about 10 minutes. Stir in the tarragon. Season with the salt and pepper. Serve hot.

DAIRY VARIATION

Just before serving, stir 1 tablespoon unsalted butter into the saucepan to enrich the sauce.

escarole with toasted bread crumbs

MAKES 4 TO 6 SERVINGS

The Nathans are passionate about garlic, and the more the better. This recipe, which we could eat as a side dish every night, is loaded with the stuff, but notice that the garlic is gently cooked to release its bold flavor. If cooked too quickly, it will be harsh. Escarole, a green that can accompany many main courses (see Herbed Turkey Patties on Braised Escarole on page 92), needs to have its profile raised in the American kitchen as it is a tasty, reasonably priced vegetable. When you're in a rush, the toasted bread crumbs are optional, but they do add a delicious crunch to the tender escarole.

Two 12-ounce heads escarole

¼ cup extra-virgin olive oil

10 garlic cloves, sliced

⅛ teaspoon hot red pepper flakes

Kosher salt and freshly ground black pepper, to taste

½ cup Toasted Bread Crumbs (page 172)

1. Trim the tough ends from the escarole. Cut each head crosswise into 2-inch-wide strips, then coarsely chop the leaves. Wash well in a large bowl or sink of cold water. Lift out and transfer to a colander, leaving any grit behind in the bottom of the bowl. Do not spin the escarole dry.

2. Meanwhile, put the oil, garlic, and red pepper flakes in a large saucepan. Cook over low heat, stirring often, until the garlic is very pale gold, about 10 minutes.

3. Increase the heat to medium-high, and immediately stir in the escarole. Cover and cook, stirring often, until the escarole is entirely wilted, about 6 minutes. Season with salt and pepper.

4. Transfer the escarole to a serving bowl and serve hot, with a bowl of the bread crumbs passed on the side for sprinkling over each portion.

PAREVE VARIATION

Omit the butter and double the oil when preparing Toasted Bread Crumbs.

orzo and garbanzos

MAKES 8 SIDE-DISH OR 4 MAIN-COURSE SERVINGS

This versatile dish can serve as a simple side dish or as a slightly more complex main course with the addition of spinach, Parmesan cheese, and pine nuts. It can also be cut in half for smaller families. When I have it, I use fresh oregano (which has a less sharp, more herbaceous flavor than dried) as a garnish, but parsley serves well, too.

12 garlic cloves, coarsely chopped

¼ cup olive oil

1 teaspoon dried oregano

One 19-ounce can garbanzo beans with their liquid

1 pound orzo

1 tablespoon chopped fresh oregano or parsley

Kosher salt and freshly ground black pepper to taste

1. Bring a large pot of lightly salted water to a boil over high heat.

2. Meanwhile, combine the garlic and oil in a large saucepan over low heat. Cook, stirring occasionally, until the garlic is golden, about 5 minutes. Stir in the dried oregano, then the beans and their liquid. Bring to a simmer over medium-high heat. Cook until the garbanzos are heated through, about 2 minutes. Set aside and keep warm.

3. Meanwhile, add the pasta to the water and cook until barely tender, about 7 minutes. Drain the pasta well. Stir into the simmering beans. Add the fresh oregano, and season with salt and pepper. Serve hot.

DAIRY VARIATION

For main-course pasta, make the dish as directed. Right before serving, add 2 cups packed shredded fresh spinach leaves, ¼ cup toasted pine nuts, and 3 tablespoons fresh Parmesan cheese. Mix well.

my kim chee

MAKES 6 TO 8 SERVINGS

I wanted to make kim chee, that spicy-sweet Korean pickled cabbage, as a side dish for my Korean-Style Short Ribs (page 108). The traditional method calls for a long fermentation period and special red pepper flakes, which posed a bit of a problem. Being a hands-on, can-do kind of guy, I came up with this Americanized version, and it's a winner. While this makes a fairly large amount, I want to encourage you to store the leftovers in the refrigerator to serve as a side dish for sandwiches, just like you would any other pickle—it will keep for a week.

1 large head bok choy, ends trimmed, leaves and stems coarsely chopped

1 medium head napa cabbage, cored and coarsely chopped

2 tablespoons kosher salt

⅓ cup rice vinegar

⅓ cup sugar

2 tablespoons dark Asian sesame oil

1 generous tablespoon minced fresh ginger

¼ teaspoon hot red pepper flakes

3 tablespoons vegetable oil, such as canola or soy

8 scallions, white and green parts, thinly sliced on the diagonal

1 canned roasted red bell pepper, chopped

¼ cup finely chopped garlic (you can use the store-bought chopped garlic in a jar)

1 tablespoon paprika, preferably Hungarian (use hot paprika, if you prefer)

1 jalapeño, seeds and ribs removed, finely chopped

1 teaspoon hot red pepper sauce, optional

1. Bring a large pot of lightly salted water to a boil over high heat. Immerse the bok choy and cabbage and stir for 30 seconds, being sure that the greens are blanched and wilted. Drain in a large colander and rinse under cold running water; leave the cabbage in the colander. Add the salt and toss well. Place a pot on the cabbage and fill it with some water to weigh the cabbage down. Let stand in the sink for 1 hour.

2. Meanwhile, whisk the vinegar, sugar, sesame oil, ginger, and red pepper flakes in a medium bowl, being sure to dissolve the sugar. Set aside.

3. A handful at a time, squeeze out as much liquid as possible from the cabbage. Heat the vegetable oil in a large skillet over medium heat. Add the scallions, red pepper, garlic, paprika, and jalapeño. Stir until the scallions wilt, about 2 minutes. Remove from the heat. Add the cabbage and the vinegar mixture, and use kitchen tongs to lift and mix the ingredients well. Cool to room temperature, or cover and refrigerate until chilled. Refrigerate for up to 1 week.

spicy oven fries

MAKES 6 TO 8 SERVINGS

When you want some crispy fries to go alongside a steak or chops, but you don't want to drag out the deep-fryer, you can't do any better than these. Parcook the potatoes in the microwave before slicing, and they'll take much less time to bake.

5 large baking potatoes, such as Burbank or russet, scrubbed but unpeeled

¼ cup olive oil

2 teaspoons sweet paprika

1 teaspoon kosher salt

1 teaspoon garlic powder

1 teaspoon onion powder

½ teaspoon dried oregano

¼ teaspoon freshly ground black pepper

⅛ teaspoon cayenne pepper

1. Pierce each potato in a few places with a fork. Microwave on high for 8 minutes; the potatoes will still feel somewhat firm. Cool completely.

2. Position a rack in the center of the oven and preheat to 400°F. Cut each potato lengthwise into 6 wedges. Spread on a large rimmed nonstick baking sheet (the potatoes will brown best if they aren't crowded) and toss with the oil. Mix the paprika, salt, garlic powder, onion powder, oregano, black pepper, and cayenne in a small bowl. Sprinkle over the potatoes and toss again to coat the potatoes evenly with the spices.

3. Bake for 10 minutes. Turn the potatoes with a metal spatula and bake 10 minutes more. Serve hot.

hummus and roasted garlic mashed potatoes

MAKES 6 TO 8 SERVINGS

My friend Rick calls me the Mashed Potato King and I suppose he's right. I love mashed potatoes and I'm always thinking up new ways to make them even better than they are in their unadorned state. Take this recipe, for example: with store-bought hummus and roasted garlic it has the added advantage of being packed with flavor, but not loaded with butter or other dairy products.

8 large baking potatoes, such as Burbank or russet, peeled and cut in halves crosswise

¾ cup store-bought hummus, at room temperature

¼ cup coarsely chopped Roasted Garlic (see sidebar), or use store-bought roasted garlic

¼ cup fresh lemon juice

¼ cup olive oil

¼ cup coarsely chopped parsley

½ teaspoon sweet paprika

¼ cup Vegetable Broth (page 44) or vegetable bouillon

Kosher salt and freshly ground black pepper to taste

1. Place the potatoes in a large pot, add enough cold salted water to cover by 1 inch, and bring to a boil over high heat. Reduce the heat to medium and cook until the potatoes are tender, 20 to 30 minutes. Drain well.

2. Return the potatoes to the same pot. Using a potato masher or an electric hand mixer, mash the potatoes to break them up. Add the hummus, chopped garlic, lemon juice, oil, parsley, and paprika and mash until smooth, beating in the broth to provide your desired consistency. Season with salt and pepper.

Roasted Garlic

Pinch a chef, and you'll get a recipe for roasted garlic. There are many different ways to do it, but I prefer a long, slow method because it gives you better control over the process. Some supermarkets even carry jars of roasted garlic. Here's how to roast your own, my way:

Peel large, plump garlic cloves. Place them in a small, shallow baking dish and add enough olive oil to cover completely. Cover tightly with aluminum foil. Bake in a preheated 200°F oven until the cloves are golden and tender, about 1 hour. Cool completely in the oil, then remove the garlic.

Be sure to save the garlicky oil for salad dressings and cooking. Refrigerate the garlic oil in a covered container for up to 1 month. It will become cloudy and semifirm when chilled, but it will liquefy again at room temperature.

curried yellow rice with almonds and currants

MAKES 4 SERVINGS

When the main course is something on the plain side, make dinner more interesting with this side dish of colorful spicy rice, inspired by the flavors of Indian cooking. The almonds and currants add crunch and bit of sweetness, but they are optional if you don't have them in the house. Try this with grilled fish or chicken breasts.

2 tablespoons olive oil

½ cup chopped onion

½ jalapeño, seeds and ribs removed, finely chopped

1 cup basmati rice

1 teaspoon curry powder

¼ teaspoon turmeric

2 cups Vegetable Broth (page 44) or use store-bought vegetable bouillon, prepared according to package instructions

½ teaspoon kosher salt

1 scallion, white and green parts, finely chopped

2 tablespoons dried currants

2 tablespoons slivered almonds, toasted (see page 180)

1. Heat the oil in a medium saucepan over medium heat. Add the onion and jalapeño and cook, stirring often, until the onion is translucent, about 5 minutes.

2. Add the basmati rice, curry powder, and turmeric and cook, stirring often, until the rice loses its glossy look, about 2 minutes. Stir in the broth and salt and bring to a boil over high heat. Reduce the heat to medium-low and cover the pot tightly. Cook until the rice is tender and has absorbed the broth, about 18 minutes. Remove from the heat and let stand for 5 minutes.

3. Fluff the rice with a fork, and mix in the scallion, currants, and almonds. Serve hot.

roasted root vegetable mash

MAKES ABOUT 8 SERVINGS

Who says that mashed veggies have to be boiled? Roasting intensifies the sweetness in root vegetables, which I play up with honey and balance with fresh herbs and lemon zest. This recipe makes a generous amount, all the better for leftovers.

2 pounds large carrots, peeled and cut into 1-inch cubes

2 pounds large parsnips, peeled and cut into 1-inch cubes

¼ cup honey

¼ cup extra-virgin olive oil

2 tablespoons chopped fresh parsley

1 tablespoon chopped fresh rosemary

Grated zest of 2 lemons

Kosher salt and freshly ground black pepper to taste

1. Position a rack in the center of the oven and preheat the oven to 350°F. Lightly oil a large rimmed baking sheet.

2. Spread the carrots and parsnips on the baking sheet. Add 1 cup water, honey, oil, parsley, rosemary, and lemon zest. Season with salt and pepper to taste. Mix well to coat the vegetables.

3. Roast, stirring occasionally, until the vegetables are tender, about 40 minutes. Scrape everything on the sheet into a large bowl and cool for a few minutes to allow some of the steam to escape (this improves the texture of the mash). Mash with a potato masher or electric hand mixer. Season again with salt and pepper as needed. Serve hot.

roasted and smashed
sweet potatoes

MAKES 4 SERVINGS

I cook a lot with sweet potatoes. Not only are they delicious, they also bring a splash of color to the plate. They don't have to be cloyingly sweet—in fact, their sugary aspect is balanced here with dill and lemon zest. For the brightest flavor and hue, look for the orange-fleshed varieties, also called yams, such as Louisiana, jewel, or garnet. The true sweet potato has slight purple cast to the skin, and a more bland yellow flesh.

4 large orange-fleshed sweet potatoes

2 tablespoons olive oil

2 tablespoons chopped fresh dill

Grated zest of 1 large lemon

1 teaspoon honey

Kosher salt and freshly ground black pepper to taste

1. Position a rack in the center of the oven and preheat to 400°F. Place the sweet potatoes on a rimmed baking sheet. Bake until they are tender, about 1 hour.

2. Protecting your hands with a kitchen towel, peel the potatoes while they are still hot and put the flesh in a medium bowl. Mash them with a potato masher.

3. Using a rubber spatula, fold in the olive oil, dill, lemon zest, and honey. Season with salt and pepper. Serve hot.

sweet potato–sweet pepper hash

MAKES 4 TO 6 SERVINGS

Sweet and spicy is a combination that my kids find irresistible, and this is one of their favorite variations on the theme. It's a kind of sweet potatoes O'Brian, jazzed up with extra spices. You can serve it as a supper side dish, or even as part of a brunch with grilled pastrami, salami, or omelets.

4 large orange-fleshed sweet potatoes, such as Louisiana, jewel, or garnet

¼ cup olive oil

2 medium onions, chopped

1 red bell pepper, cored, seeded, and finely chopped

1 green bell pepper, cored, seeded, and finely chopped

1 jalapeño, seeds and ribs discarded, minced

1 tablespoon Blackened Spice Blend (page 139), or use store-bought

Kosher salt and freshly ground black pepper to taste

2 tablespoons chopped fresh cilantro

1 tablespoon fresh lime juice

1. Position a rack in the center of the oven and preheat to 400°F. Place the sweet potatoes on a baking sheet. Bake until the potatoes are just tender when pierced with the tip of a thin sharp knife, but not soft, about 50 minutes. Cool until easy to handle. Peel the sweet potatoes and cut the flesh into 1-inch dice.

2. Heat the oil in a large skillet over medium heat. Add the onions, red and green bell peppers, and jalapeño. Cook, stirring occasionally, until the vegetables begin to soften, about 10 minutes. Add the sweet potatoes and spice blend and cook, stirring occasionally, until the edges of the sweet potatoes are browned, about 10 minutes more. Season with salt and pepper.

3. Remove from the heat and stir in the cilantro and lime juice. Serve hot.

green beans with sun-dried tomato, olive, and thyme butter

MAKES 6 SERVINGS

This is a fine example of why I think everyone should have logs of compound butter in their freezer. With the addition of a few tablespoons of the intense sun-dried tomato and olive butter, plain old green beans go on a Roman holiday! Try this technique—a quick blanch, a fast sauté, and a finish with flavored butter—on other vegetables, such as zucchini, broccoli, and asparagus.

1 pound green beans, trimmed and cut into 1½-inch lengths

¼ cup olive oil

6 cloves garlic, sliced

4 tablespoons Sun-Dried Tomato, Olive, and Thyme Butter (recipe follows),
    cut into 4 or more pats

Kosher salt and freshly ground black pepper to taste

1. Bring a large saucepan of lightly salted water to a boil over high heat. Add the green beans and cook just until they turn bright green, about 1½ minutes. Drain and rinse under cold water. (The green beans can be prepared up to 8 hours ahead, wrapped in paper towels, stored in a plastic bag, and refrigerated.)

2. Heat the oil and garlic in a large skillet over low heat until the garlic turns golden brown, about 6 minutes. Add the green beans and increase the heat to medium. Top with the butter. Cook, stirring occasionally, until the green beans are heated through and the butter is melted, 2 to 3 minutes. Season with salt and pepper. Serve hot.

Sun-Dried Tomato, Olive, and Thyme Butter

MAKES ABOUT 1½ CUPS

I use this butter most often as a way to perk up simply prepared vegetables. But, it is also great tossed with pasta and goat cheese as a quick meal (add some vegetable broth or water to help moisten the pasta, too). And I can't forget to tell you about using it to dress up grilled or broiled fish fillets.

1 cup (2 sticks) unsalted butter, softened

¼ cup coarsely chopped pitted kalamata olives

¼ cup coarsely chopped sun-dried tomatoes

2 tablespoons chopped fresh thyme

Zest of 1 lemon

1½ tablespoons fresh lemon juice

½ teaspoon kosher salt

¼ teaspoon freshly ground black pepper

1. Using an electric mixer on medium speed (I prefer a standing mixer with a paddle blade for this recipe, but a hand mixer will work, too), beat the butter in a medium bowl until it is light and fluffy, about 2 minutes. Add the olives, sun-dried tomatoes, thyme, lemon zest, lemon juice, salt, and pepper and mix well.

2. Place an 18-inch square of plastic wrap on your work surface. Scrape the butter out onto the wrap, about 2 inches from the bottom edge, shaping the butter into a rough strip about 12 inches long and 2 inches wide. Fold the bottom edge of the plastic wrap over to cover the butter. Roll up the plastic wrap to shape the butter into a cylinder. Pick up the cylinder by the two ends of plastic wrap. Twist the ends of the wrap, and it will tighten to shape the butter into a compact log (see photographs on page 131). Refrigerate the butter until it is firm, at least 2 hours. (The butter can be made up to 1 week ahead, refrigerated. To freeze the butter, wrap the log, still in the plastic wrap, in aluminum foil and freeze for up to 3 months.)

desserts

We don't take desserts for granted in our house. There are no super-sized jars of factory-made cookies for careless snacking. Desserts are a special treat, and so they must be fantastic.

Many of our favorite desserts are made with fresh fruit, which is a fine way to get the kids to enjoy healthful eating. The Pineapple "Shekels" with Tropical Fruits (page 229) and Poached Apricots with Lemon and Thyme (page 213) are two fruit-based sweets that we can serve year-round. Ice cream does find its way into our freezer often enough, and the Banana-Butterscotch Sundae (page 216) is a simple way to dress it up. We all like it when a bowl of homemade rice pudding (page 230) is in the refrigerator.

Desserts are an important part of holiday cooking, and I just had to share some of our family's favorites. At Hanukkah, we always make the Apple Latkes (page 214) together. And you're guaranteed a sweet New Year when you make Taeglach (page 232). The kids get involved with that one, too. The Lemon Sponge Cake with Strawberry Cream (page 226) is a sure-fire winner at Passover. And when a family member requests a chocolate birthday cake, the one on page 222 could not be easier.

A few of these desserts include a very small amount of liquor or wine. I feel that my kids should be exposed to these flavors as adolescents so that there isn't a taboo attached to alcohol. If you are serving the desserts to a group of adults, or if your children are old enough to consume alcohol without your concern, some recipes have spiked versions.

Remember, there are calories, and then there are *quality* calories. If you are going to indulge in desserts, let them be as good as these.

almond mini muffins

MAKES ABOUT 2 DOZEN MINI MUFFINS

Most families who keep kosher kitchens have a can of almond paste around to make macaroons at Passover, but there are many more uses for this wonderful ingredient. We make these great mini muffins when the kids' friends come over for a visit, and they immediately disappear. They are quite sweet and dense (like a cookie), so resist the temptation to make them any larger. The oven temperature is unusually low, but correct, since a higher temperature would burn these rich morsels.

One 8-ounce can almond paste

¾ cup confectioners' sugar, plus more for decorating

¾ cup all-purpose flour

3 tablespoons vegetable shortening

2 large eggs, at room temperature

12 whole almonds, split in half

1. Position a rack in the center of the oven and preheat to 300°F. Line 24 mini muffin cups (2 tablespoon capacity) with paper mini baking cups.

2. Beat the almond paste, ¾ cup confectioners' sugar, flour, and shortening in a heavy-duty electric mixer with the paddle blade on medium speed until the mixture is well combined, about 5 minutes. One at a time, beat in the eggs.

3. Transfer the batter to a pastry bag without a tube. (Or use a 1-gallon plastic bag, and snip off one end with scissors to make an opening about 1 inch wide.) Pipe the batter into the muffin cups. Place an almond half on each muffin.

4. Bake until the muffins are lightly browned and feel set when pressed with a finger, about 45 minutes. Cool in the pan for 5 minutes. Transfer the muffins in their paper cups to a wire cake rack and cool completely. Sift a little confectioners' sugar over the muffins and serve.

poached apricots with lemon and thyme

MAKES 6 TO 8 SERVINGS

We have most of these ingredients in the pantry, so it's a simple matter to make this dessert when the mood strikes. The taste of thyme in a dessert may be surprising, but it is as delicious as it is aromatic. And be sure to use freshly grated nutmeg (is there any other kind?). We often serve the apricots without the ice cream as a compote.

2 lemons

½ cup fresh orange juice

½ cup honey

¼ cup sugar

One 3-inch cinnamon stick

1 pound dried apricots

1 tablespoon chopped fresh thyme

A few gratings of fresh nutmeg

Vanilla ice cream, for serving

1. Grate the lemon zest from 1 lemon. Juice this lemon and strain the juice. Using a vegetable peeler, remove the zest from the second lemon and cut the zest lengthwise into thin strips (julienne). Reserve the second lemon for another use.

2. Mix 2 cups water, the orange juice, honey, sugar, grated lemon zest, lemon juice, and cinnamon in a medium saucepan. Add the apricots and bring to a simmer over medium heat, stirring occasionally. Partially cover the saucepan with the lid, and simmer until the apricots are tender, about 10 minutes.

3. Remove from the heat and add the thyme and nutmeg. Cool until warm (or cool, cover, and refrigerate until chilled). Serve spooned over ice cream and topped with julienned lemon zest.

VARIATION: POACHED APRICOTS WITH AMARETTO

In step 3, add ¼ cup almond-flavored liqueur, such as Amaretto di Saronno, to the poaching liquid with the thyme.

apple latkes with spiced sour cream

MAKES 4 TO 5 SERVINGS

Fried food at Hanukkah commemorates the miraculous burning of the oil in the ancient Temple of Jerusalem, and latkes are the culinary tradition. Instead of the potato variety, we often make these sweet fritters as dessert or an indulgent supper. The end of our local apple season coincides with the holiday, so these are also an edible farewell to autumn. Be sure to use apples that hold their shape during cooking— Golden Delicious, Fuji, and Granny Smith all work well, but McIntosh and Red Delicious become mushy.

Spiced Sour Cream

One 8-ounce container sour cream

$\frac{1}{2}$ teaspoon vanilla extract

$\frac{1}{4}$ teaspoon ground cinnamon, or more to taste

$1\frac{1}{2}$ cups all-purpose flour

$\frac{1}{2}$ cup granulated sugar

$\frac{3}{4}$ teaspoon baking powder

1 teaspoon ground cinnamon

$\frac{1}{4}$ teaspoon ground allspice

$\frac{3}{4}$ cup water

2 firm apples, such as Golden Delicious, Fuji, or Granny Smith, unpeeled

$\frac{1}{2}$ cup canola oil, as needed

Confectioners' sugar, for sprinkling

1. To make the spiced sour cream, stir together the sour cream, vanilla, and cinnamon in a small bowl. Set aside at room temperature while making the latkes so it can lose its chill.

2. Whisk the flour, sugar, baking powder, cinnamon, and allspice in a medium bowl. Whisk in the water until barely smooth.

3. Core the apples and cut into $\frac{1}{4}$-inch dice. Immediately fold the diced apples into the batter.

4. Line a baking sheet with a double thickness of paper towels. Heat the oil over high heat until it begins to shimmer. Reduce the heat to medium. Working in batches, using about $^1/_3$ cup for each latke, pour the batter into the skillet. Cook until the underside is golden brown, about $1^1/_2$ minutes, adjusting the heat as needed so the latkes don't burn. Turn and cook the other side. Transfer to the paper towels to drain briefly. It is best to serve each batch immediately after draining. If you wish, use two skillets to keep them coming at a fast pace.

5. Sprinkle the latkes with confectioners' sugar. Serve at once, with the sour cream passed on the side.

PAREVE VARIATION

Do not serve the spiced sour cream.

banana-butterscotch sundae

MAKES 4 SERVINGS

When you have neighbors over for a visit, it's nice to serve something sweet. We usually have bananas on the kitchen counter and ice cream in the freezer, so this sundae is easy to throw together. When the kids aren't around, indulge in the dark-rum-and-liqueur-spiked variation.

1 cup (2 sticks) unsalted butter

½ teaspoon ground cinnamon

Four 3-inch cinnamon sticks, optional

⅓ cup packed light or dark brown sugar

4 ripe bananas, cut into ½-inch-thick rounds

¼ cup coarsely chopped walnuts

⅓ cup apple juice

1½ pints vanilla ice cream

1. Place the butter, cinnamon, and cinnamon sticks, if using, in a large skillet. Melt the butter over medium heat. Add the sugar and stir until the sugar dissolves.

2. Add the sliced bananas and mix well. Stir in the walnuts and apple juice. Cook, stirring constantly, until the syrup is lightly thickened, about 2 minutes. Remove the cinnamon sticks and set aside. Let the banana sauce cool until warm.

3. Scoop equal amounts of the ice cream into 4 bowls. Top with the warm banana sauce, and garnish each with a cinnamon stick, if desired. Serve immediately.

SPIKED BANANA-BUTTERSCOTCH SUNDAE

Substitute ¼ cup dark rum and 2 tablespoons banana liqueur for the apple juice.

sweet grilled cheese sandwich with mascarpone and orange

MAKES 6 SERVINGS

With this recipe, a container of mascarpone and store-bought pound cake can create a sophisticated but simple dessert in no time. It will melt in your mouth and quickly become a family favorite. It's an all-season dessert that can be varied by the fresh fruit on the plate, from grapes and orange slices in winter to summer berries.

Mascarpone-Orange Cream

8 ounces mascarpone

Grated zest of $\frac{1}{2}$ orange

1 tablespoon confectioners' sugar

1 tablespoon honey

$\frac{1}{4}$ teaspoon vanilla extract

One 1-pound "all butter" pound cake, cut crosswise into 16 slices

9 tablespoons (1 stick plus 1 tablespoon) unsalted butter, softened

Fresh fruit, such as grape clusters and raspberries, for serving

1. To make the mascarpone cream, combine the mascarpone, orange zest, confectioners' sugar, honey, and vanilla in a medium bowl with a rubber spatula just until combined. Do not overwork the mascarpone, or it will separate.

2. If you wish, trim the crusts from the cake slices so the slices are square. Spread the mascarpone cream on 6 cake slices, and top with the remaining 6 slices to make sandwiches. Spread the tops of the sandwiches with the 8 tablespoons of butter. (The sandwiches can be covered with plastic wrap and chilled for up to 3 hours.)

3. Melt the remaining 1 tablespoon butter in a very large skillet over medium heat. Place the sandwiches on the skillet, buttered sides down. Grill until the undersides are toasted, 2 to 3 minutes. Turn and toast the other sides, about 2 minutes more.

4. Cut each sandwich diagonally in half to make triangles. Place two triangles on each dessert plate, garnish with fresh fruit, and serve.

cannoli blintzes

MAKES 4 TO 6 SERVINGS

Several years ago, when making cheese blintzes for supper, I realized their similarity to Italian cannoli—both had a creamy cheese filling and both were wrapped up. The next time I made blintzes, I went further with the Italian inspiration, and they ended up sweet enough to serve for dessert. Be sure to use a firm ricotta, otherwise the blintzes will be soggy. If you have any doubts, place the ricotta in a paper towel–lined sieve, place a plate on top, and let it drain over a bowl for 30 minutes or so to remove the excess whey. Unlike farmer's cheese, the ricotta filling has a tendency to separate when frozen, so don't freeze these blintzes.

Crêpes

8 tablespoons (1 stick) unsalted butter

¾ cup plus 2 tablespoons milk, plus more as needed

½ cup water

2 large eggs

1 cup plus 2 tablespoons all-purpose flour

A pinch of kosher salt

2 tablespoons vegetable oil

Filling

One 15-ounce container ricotta cheese

2 large egg yolks

¼ cup confectioners' sugar

¾ teaspoon rum extract

Grated zest of ½ orange

Garnish

2 ounces bittersweet chocolate, in a chunk

Confectioners' sugar, for sifting

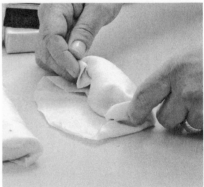

1. To make the crêpes, cook the butter in a small saucepan over medium heat until it melts and comes to a boil. Pour the melted butter into a small bowl and let stand for a few minutes. Spoon off the clear yellow clarified butter and transfer it to another small bowl. Discard the milky residue in the first bowl.

2. Whisk the milk, water, eggs, and 2 tablespoons of the clarified butter in a medium bowl. Whisk in the flour and salt, just until the batter is barely smooth. Mix the vegetable oil into the remaining clarified butter.

3. Dip a crumpled paper towel into the butter-oil mixture, and use it to coat the the inside of a 7½- to 8-inch diameter nonstick skillet. Heat the skillet over medium-high heat until hot, about 1½ minutes. Pour a scant ¼ cup of the batter into the bottom of the skillet and immediately tilt and swirl the skillet so the batter coats the bottom in a thin layer. Cook until the edges look dry and the top is set, about 1 minute. Using a heatproof spatula, lift and turn the crêpe. Cook until splotched with golden-brown spots, about 30 seconds. Transfer to a plate. Repeat with the remaining batter, wiping the pan with butter-oil each time. Separate the crêpes as you stack them with pieces of waxed paper between. (The crêpes can be prepared 1 day ahead, stacked, and covered with plastic wrap.) Reserve the remaining butter-oil mixture.

4. To make the filling, mix the ricotta, egg yolks, confectioners' sugar, rum extract, and orange zest in a medium bowl until combined.

5. To assemble the blintzes, place a crêpe, spotted side up, on the work surface. Spread about 3 tablespoons of the filling in a strip about 1 inch from the bottom and sides of the crêpe. Fold the bottom edge up to cover the filling. Fold in the right side about 1 inch, repeat with the left side, and roll up. Place seam side down on a baking sheet. Repeat with the remaining crêpes and filling. Cover with plastic wrap and refrigerate until ready to serve, up to 2 hours.

6. To cook the blintzes, preheat the oven to 200°F. Heat about 2½ tablespoons of the butter-oil mixture in a large skillet over medium heat until very hot. Add 6 blintzes and cook, turning occasionally and adjusting the heat as necessary to keep the blintzes from burning, until the blintzes are crisp and golden brown, about 5 minutes. (Traditional blintzes are soft, but these should have a crisper texture.) Transfer the cooked blintzes to a baking sheet and keep warm in the oven. Repeat with the remaining blintzes and butter-oil mixture.

7. To serve, transfer the blintzes to a platter. Using a box grater, grate the chocolate on top. Sift confectioners' sugar over the blintzes and serve hot.

chocolate drops

MAKES ABOUT 2 DOZEN DROPS

Make these for Passover, or any time of the year when you want something sweet around the house. For a more elegant presentation, drop the melted chocolate mixture into lightly oiled mini muffin cups. If you make the drops with milk chocolate, they will become dairy.

¼ cup unsweetened shredded coconut

1 pound semisweet chocolate, finely chopped

1¼ cups (5 ounces) unsalted roasted cashews, coarsely crushed

½ cup golden raisins

1. Position a rack in the center of the oven and preheat the oven to 350°F. Line a baking sheet with parchment paper or waxed paper.

2. Spread the coconut on an unlined baking sheet. Bake, stirring occasionally, until the coconut is toasted, about 10 minutes. Cool completely.

3. Melt the chocolate in the top part of a double boiler set over barely simmering water. Remove the insert from the heat. Stir in the cashews and raisins.

4. Drop the chocolate mixture by tablespoons onto the parchment paper to make about 2 dozen mounds. Sprinkle each with toasted coconut. Chill until ready to serve.

chocolate-orange fondue

MAKES 6 TO 8 SERVINGS

You can practically make this dessert with your eyes closed. Just about every market carries kosher milk chocolate bars with orange "creme" filling. Melted with heavy cream, these bars make an incredible chocolate fondue. For serving, use a small 1- to 2-cup ceramic fondue pot (available at kitchenware shops), because this fondue is so rich you won't need a larger pot.

¾ cup heavy cream
Four 3½-ounce orange-filled milk chocolate candy bars
Cookies, large strawberries with their stems, and chunks of pound cake, for serving

1. Bring the cream to a simmer in a medium saucepan over medium heat. Transfer to the top part of a double boiler set over medium heat. (If your double boiler insert is flameproof, heat the cream in the insert over medium heat.)

2. Working over the double boiler, break up the chocolate bars into pieces, letting the pieces fall into the hot cream. (If you chop them on a cutting board, you'll leave most of the candy bar on the board.) Let stand until the chocolate has melted, about 3 minutes.

3. Transfer to a small ceramic fondue pot and keep warm over a burner. Serve immediately with the cookies, strawberries, and cake, for dipping.

VARIATION: SPIKED CHOCOLATE-ORANGE FONDUE

Add 2 tablespoons orange liqueur, such as Triple Sec, to the fondue with the chocolate.

chocolate mayonnaise cake with easy cocoa frosting

MAKES 12 SERVINGS

This chocolate cake has been around for ages, but every time I make it, people are surprised to discover the secret of its moist texture—mayonnaise. If you think about it, it's not that surprising, as eggs and oil are mayonnaise's main components. The real surprise is how easy it is to make, and no creaming butter or separating eggs. Because it's so moist, the cake keeps longer than most, and is perfect for snacking and for tucking into lunch boxes.

Cake

2 cups all-purpose flour

1 cup granulated sugar

$\frac{1}{3}$ cup plus 1 tablespoon cocoa powder (not Dutch processed)

2 teaspoons baking soda

$\frac{1}{4}$ teaspoon salt

1 cup mayonnaise

1 cup cold strong brewed coffee

1 teaspoon vanilla extract

Frosting

$1\frac{1}{4}$ cups confectioners' sugar

$\frac{2}{3}$ cup cocoa powder (not Dutch processed)

3 tablespoons unsalted butter, at room temperature

$\frac{1}{3}$ cup heavy cream

$\frac{1}{2}$ teaspoon vanilla extract

1. To make the cake: Position a rack in the center of the oven and preheat to 350°F. Lightly butter a 13 × 9-inch baking pan. Dust the inside with flour and tap out the excess flour.

2. Sift the flour, sugar, cocoa, baking soda, and salt into a medium bowl and make a well in the center. In another bowl, whisk the mayonnaise, coffee, and vanilla. Pour into the well. Mix with an electric mixer on low speed, scraping down the sides of the bowl as needed, just until the batter is smooth; do not overbeat. Pour the batter into the pan and smooth the top.

3. Bake until a wooden toothpick inserted into the center of the cake comes out clean, about 30 minutes. Transfer to a wire cake rack and cool completely.

4. To make the frosting: Sift the confectioners' sugar and cocoa onto a piece of waxed paper. Beat the butter with an electric mixer in a medium bowl on low speed. Using the wax paper as a funnel, gradually add the sugar-cocoa mixture, alternating with the heavy cream, and beat until smooth. You may use more or less cream to reach the desired consistency. Beat in the vanilla.

5. Spread the frosting over the top of the cake. Cut into squares to serve. (The cake will keep for up to 3 days, covered tightly with plastic wrap and stored at room temperature.)

lemon bars

MAKES 12 BARS

There are plenty of recipes for lemon bars out there, but these are especially tart with a rich, buttery crust. A family can eat only so many lemon bars, so surprise your coworkers with the leftovers.

Crust

½ cup granulated sugar

6 tablespoons (¾ stick) unsalted butter, at room temperature

2 cups all-purpose flour

1 tablespoon ice water, or as needed

Filling

6 large eggs

1½ cups granulated sugar

Grated zest of 1 lemon

⅔ cup fresh lemon juice

1 teaspoon baking powder

Pinch of kosher salt

1. Position a rack in the center of the oven and preheat to 350°F. Lightly butter and flour a 13 × 9-inch baking pan.

2. To make the crust, beat the sugar and butter in a medium bowl with an electric mixer on high speed until the mixture is light in color and texture, about 3 minutes. Reduce the speed to low. Add the flour and mix until the mixture forms fine crumbs. Sprinkle with the water and mix on low speed until the dough clumps together. Add more water, a teaspoon at a time, if the dough is too dry. Press the dough evenly in the pan.

3. Bake until the edges of the dough are pale gold, about 15 minutes. Cool completely.

4. To make the filling, beat the eggs in a medium bowl with the electric mixer on high speed until the eggs are evenly colored and foamy. Add the sugar, lemon zest, lemon juice, baking powder, and salt and beat until blended. Pour into the cooled crust.

5. Bake until the filling is set, about 25 minutes. Cool completely on a wire rack.

6. Cut into bars and lift out of the pan with a spatula. (The bars can be stored for up to 3 days, individually wrapped in plastic wrap and refrigerated.)

lemon sponge cake
with strawberry cream

MAKES 12 SERVINGS

When Passover comes around, cooks scramble for their best flour-free desserts. This light-textured cake never fails to please and celebrates the season with fresh spring berries. The cake is baked in an angel food cake pan, and while there are many on the market, be sure to use one that does not have a coated or nonstick interior, or the batter will not rise to its full height. Also, note that the cake is cooled upside down to set its delicate structure. Most angel food cake pans now have small feet that will keep the cake from touching the work surface. If your pan lacks feet, balance the edges of the pan on the edges of three coffee mugs of the same height.

Cake

8 large eggs, separated, at room temperature

1⅓ cups sugar

Grated zest of 2 lemons

3 tablespoons fresh lemon juice

½ teaspoon kosher salt

¾ cup potato starch

Strawberry Cream

1 pint fresh strawberries, hulled and coarsely chopped

2 tablespoons sugar

One 8-ounce container nondairy whipped topping

1. To make the cake, position a rack in the center of the oven and preheat to 350°F.

2. In a large bowl, using an electric mixer on high speed, beat the egg whites until they form soft peaks. One tablespoon at a time, beat in ⅔ cup sugar until the whites are stiff and shiny, but not dry. Set aside.

3. Beat the egg yolks and the remaining ⅔ cup sugar in another large bowl until the yolks are very thick and form a ribbon when the beaters are lifted a few inches above the yolks, about 3 minutes. Beat in the lemon zest and juice, and salt. Sift the potato starch over the yolks and fold it in with a large spatula, leaving a few wisps of potato starch visible. Stir one-fourth of the whites into the batter to lighten it. Scoop the remaining whites on top and fold them in, just until the batter is combined. Spread the batter evenly in an ungreased 10-inch angel food cake pan with a removable insert.

4. Bake until the cake springs back when pressed lightly with your fingers, about 45 minutes. Turn the cake upside down and cool completely, at least 4 hours. (The cake can be made 1 day ahead, covered loosely in plastic wrap and stored at room temperature.)

5. Meanwhile, make the strawberry cream. Combine the strawberries and sugar in a medium bowl. Cover and refrigerate until the berries release their juices, at least 4 hours or overnight. Drain the berries, reserving the juices. Transfer the topping to a serving bowl. Fold the berries into the topping, adding enough of the juices to color the topping without thinning it too much. (The strawberry cream can be prepared up to 1 day ahead, covered and refrigerated. If it thins upon standing, whisk well before serving.)

6. To remove the cake from the pan, slip a flexible metal spatula carefully down the side of the pan. Slowly slide the spatula around the perimeter to release the cake. When the sides are free, push up on the removable insert to remove the cake from the sides. Tilt the cake and gently pull it up and away from the bottom of the insert. Place the cake on a serving platter.

7. Using a serrated knife, cut the cake into wedges. Serve on dessert plates with a large dollop of the strawberry cream.

DAIRY VARIATION

Substitute 1¼ cups heavy cream, whipped with 3 tablespoons granulated sugar, for the whipped topping.

peanut butter chocolate chip cookies

MAKES ABOUT 2 DOZEN COOKIES

Here's something for the cookie jar, especially for those families that like peanut butter and chocolate combinations—in my experience, that is a lot of people. (Before serving them to your kids' friends, be sure that no one in the group is allergic to peanuts.) Get familiar with parchment paper or silicone baking mats, which eliminate the need for buttering and flouring cookie sheets. You'll never go back to the old way.

1¼ cups all-purpose flour

1 teaspoon baking soda

½ cup peanut butter

8 tablespoons (1 stick) unsalted butter, at room temperature

1 cup packed light brown sugar (see Note)

1 large egg, at room temperature

½ teaspoon vanilla extract

1 cup semisweet chocolate chips

1. Position racks in the center and top third of the oven and preheat the oven to 350°F. Line two baking sheets with parchment paper or silicone baking mats. (Or butter and flour the sheets.)

2. Sift the flour and baking soda together onto a sheet of waxed paper. Beat the peanut butter, butter, and brown sugar in a medium bowl with an electric mixer on high speed until the mixture is light in color and texture, about 3 minutes. Beat in the egg, then the vanilla. Stir in the flour mixture. Mix in the chips.

3. Moisten your hands with water. Using a tablespoon per cookie, shape the dough into balls. Place the balls 2 inches apart on the prepared sheets.

4. Bake until the cookies are lightly browned around the edges, about 15 minutes. Cool for 5 minutes on the baking sheets, then transfer to a wire cake rack and cool completely. (The cookies can be stored in an airtight container at room temperature for up to 5 days.)

NOTE The brown sugar must be absolutely lump-free to cream well with the butter. If you have any doubts, rub the sugar through a coarse wire sieve to smooth it out.

pineapple "shekels" with tropical fruits

MAKES 6 SERVINGS

Shekels is Hebrew for coins, and as the thin, bright yellow pineapple wedges remind us of coins, we call these pineapple shekels. Combined with other tropical fruits, this is a colorful and healthy dessert. If you have them, place a few ripe figs in the center of the ring of pineapple wedges before adding the fruit salad.

¼ cup pineapple juice (collected from cutting the pineapple, or use canned juice), orange juice, or sweet white wine

½ teaspoon ground cinnamon

1 ripe mango, peeled, pit removed, and coarsely chopped

1 ripe papaya, peeled, seeds removed, and coarsely chopped

4 strawberries, hulled and halved

1 cup seedless green grapes, each cut into quarters

6 pitted dates, chopped

¼ cup honey

2 tablespoons chopped fresh mint

½ ripe pineapple, pared, cored, quartered, and cut crosswise into ⅛-inch-thick wedges

1. Combine the pineapple juice and cinnamon and stir. Combine the mango, papaya, and strawberries in a food processor fitted with the metal blade and pulse until finely chopped. Transfer to the bowl with the juice and cinnamon and add the grapes, dates, honey, and mint. Toss gently to combine. Cover and refrigerate until chilled, at least 1 hour.

2. Arrange the pineapple wedges in a circle on a platter, slightly overlapping each other. Spoon the chopped fruit in another circle to cover the inside edges of the pineapple wedges. Serve chilled.

spiced rice pudding

MAKES 6 SERVINGS

Rice pudding must hold a place of honor in the Comfort Food Hall of Fame. In addition to the typical cinnamon, I like to add star anise, which has a similar, but more exotic, flavor, but it is optional. Also, for the creamiest texture, use starchy medium- or short-grain rice (such as those used for risotto or sushi, respectively) instead of firm long-grain rice.

6 cups whole milk

1 cup medium- or short-grain rice, such as arborio or Japanese-style for sushi

½ cup granulated sugar

One 3-inch cinnamon stick

1 star anise (optional)

Pinch of kosher salt

¾ cup heavy cream, plus more if needed

2 tablespoons golden raisins, soaked in hot water for 20 minutes and drained

2 tablespoons light brown sugar

1 tablespoon unsalted butter

Grated zest of 1 lemon

Sweetened whipped cream, for serving

1. Combine the milk, rice, granulated sugar, cinnamon, star anise, and salt in a heavy-bottomed medium saucepan. Bring to a simmer over medium heat, stirring often. Reduce the heat to medium-low and cook, stirring often to avoid scorching, until the rice is tender, about 30 minutes. (The sugar will inhibit the softening of the rice, so be patient, and stir often.) Stir in the heavy cream and simmer, still stirring often, until the rice is very tender and the liquid is very thick, about 15 minutes more. Stir in the raisins, brown sugar, butter, and lemon zest. Remove and discard the cinnamon stick and star anise.

2. Transfer the pudding to a medium bowl. Press a sheet of plastic wrap directly on the surface of the pudding to prevent a skin from forming, and pierce the wrap with the tip of a sharp knife to allow some steam to escape. Refrigerate until chilled, at least 4 hours. If the chilled pudding is too thick for your taste, stir in additional cream.

3. To serve, spoon the chilled pudding into dessert bowls and top with whipped cream.

VARIATION: ANISE RICE PUDDING WITH SAMBUCA

Stir 2 tablespoons Sambuca into the rice pudding along with the raisins.

taeglach

MAKES 6 TO 8 SERVINGS

For a sweet New Year, you've got to make taeglach! It is a lot of fun to roll and deep-fry the little balls of dough, and Chad and Jackie love to help out. Then it's on to heaping the balls into a mound, adding whatever goodies you feel like to the honey syrup. The amount of additional ingredients (coconut, mixed nuts, or dried fruits are popular options) is up to you, as some families like more or less than others.

Taeglach

3 large eggs

1 tablespoon unsalted butter, softened

1 tablespoon sugar

1¾ cups all-purpose flour, plus more as needed

½ teaspoon baking powder

Vegetable oil, for deep-frying

Syrup

¾ cup honey

¼ cup sugar

1 teaspoon vanilla

1 teaspoon ground cinnamon

1 to 3 cups shredded coconut, chopped mixed nuts, dried fruit, or a mixture of all three, as desired

1. To make the taeglach, fit a standing heavy-duty mixer with the paddle beater. Add the eggs, butter, and sugar to the bowl. Beat on medium speed until foamy. Sift the flour and baking powder together. On low speed, gradually add the flour to the eggs and mix to make a firm dough. If the dough seems sticky, mix in additional flour, 1 tablespoon at a time. (You can also beat the egg mixture with a hand mixer, and stir in the flour mixture by hand.)

2. Pour enough oil to come halfway up the sides of a deep saucepan. Heat over high heat until a deep-frying thermometer reads 350°F.

3. Meanwhile, dust a baking sheet with flour. Line another baking sheet with paper towels. Divide the dough into 4 equal portions. Working with one portion at a time, place the dough on a clean work surface and roll the dough under your hands into a 12-inch-long rope. Cut the rope into ½-inch-thick pieces. Transfer to the baking sheet and sprinkle with a little additional flour.

4. In batches, without crowding, shake off the excess flour, and deep-fry the dough in the oil until golden, about 2 minutes. Using a wire skimmer or slotted spoon, transfer the fried dough to the paper towels. Cool completely.

5. To make the syrup, stir the honey and sugar over medium-low heat until the sugar is melted. Simmer without stirring until the syrup thickens slightly, about 3 minutes. Remove from the heat. Stir the vanilla and cinnamon together in a small bowl, then stir into the syrup. In batches, add the fried dough to the saucepan and mix with a slotted spoon. Transfer the coated dough to the bowl. Add the coconut or other ingredients and mix to combine.

6. When cool enough to handle, turn the sticky mass onto a platter, and shape with a spoon into a free-form mound. Cool completely.

strawberries and marsala with honeyed cream

MAKES 6 SERVINGS

When I want to serve a simple but impressive dessert that takes only minutes to make, I turn to these cream-cloaked strawberries. Marsala has a caramel-like flavor that is brought out by the honey in the whipped cream. While this is spectacular with in-season, farmstand berries, the macerating does wonders for the supermarket variety, too.

3 pints strawberries

⅓ cup sweet Marsala

2 tablespoons sugar, as needed

1 cup heavy cream

¼ cup honey

Mint leaves for garnish, optional

1. Hull the strawberries, and cut them in halves or quarters, depending on their size. Combine the strawberries, Marsala, and sugar in a medium bowl and mix gently. Cover and refrigerate for at least 20 minutes and up to 1 hour, until the strawberries release their juices—the longer the berries macerate, the more juice you'll have. Stir the berries whenever you remember to do so.

2. Combine the cream and honey in a chilled medium bowl. Using an electric mixer on high, whip the cream until it forms moderately stiff peaks. Do not overbeat the cream; it should have a billowing, light, and delicate texture. (The cream can be whipped up to 1 day ahead, covered tightly with plastic wrap, and refrigerated.)

3. Spoon the strawberries and juice into parfait glasses or dessert bowls. Top with a dollop of the cream, and the mint leaves, if desired. Serve immediately.

EQUIVALENT IMPERIAL AND METRIC MEASUREMENTS

American cooks use standard containers, the 8-ounce cup and a tablespoon that takes exactly 16 level fillings to fill that cup level. Measuring by cup makes it very difficult to give weight equivalents, as a cup of densely packed butter will weigh considerably more than a cup of flour. The easiest way therefore to deal with cup measurements in recipes is to take the amount by volume rather than by weight. Thus the equation reads:

1 cup = 240 ml = 8 fl. oz. $^1\!/_2$ cup = 120 ml = 4 fl. oz.

In the States, butter is often measured in sticks. One stick is the equivalent of 8 tablespoons. One tablespoon of butter is therefore equivalent to $^1\!/_2$ ounce/15 grams.

liquid measures

Fluid Ounces	U.S.	Imperial	Milliliters
$^1\!/_8$	1 teaspoon	1 teaspoon	5
$^1\!/_4$	2 teaspoons	1 dessertspoon	10
$^1\!/_2$	1 tablespoon	1 tablespoon	14
1	2 tablespoons	2 tablespoons	28
2	$^1\!/_4$ cup	4 tablespoons	56
4	$^1\!/_2$ cup		120
5		$^1\!/_4$ pint or 1 gill	140
6	$^3\!/_4$ cup		170
8	1 cup		240
9			250, $^1\!/_4$ liter
10	$1^1\!/_4$ cups	$^1\!/_2$ pint	280
12	$1^1\!/_2$ cups		340
15		$^3\!/_4$ pint	420
16	2 cups		450
18	$2^1\!/_4$ cups		500, $^1\!/_2$ liter
20	$2^1\!/_2$ cups	1 pint	560
24	3 cups		675
25		$1^1\!/_4$ pints	700
27	$3^1\!/_2$ cups		750
30	$3^3\!/_4$ cups	$1^1\!/_2$ pints	840
32	4 cups or 1 quart		900
35		$1^3\!/_4$ pints	980
36	$4^1\!/_2$ cups		1000, 1 liter
40	5 cups	2 pints or 1 quart	1120

solid measures

U.S. and Imperial Measures		Metric Measures	
Ounces	Pounds	Grams	Kilos
1		28	
2		56	
$3^1\!/_2$		100	
4	$^1\!/_4$	112	
5		140	
6		168	
8	$^1\!/_2$	225	
9		250	$^1\!/_4$
12	$^3\!/_4$	340	
16	1	450	
18		500	$^1\!/_2$
20	$1^1\!/_4$	560	
24	$1^1\!/_2$	675	
27		750	$^3\!/_4$
28	$1^3\!/_4$	780	
32	2	900	
36	$2^1\!/_4$	1000	1
40	$2^1\!/_2$	1100	
48	3	1350	
54		1500	$1^1\!/_2$

oven temperature equivalents

Fahrenheit	Celsius	Gas Mark	Description
225	110	$^1\!/_4$	Cool
250	130	$^1\!/_2$	
275	140	1	Very Slow
300	150	2	
325	170	3	Slow
350	180	4	Moderate
375	190	5	
400	200	6	Moderately Hot
425	220	7	Fairly Hot
450	230	8	Hot
475	240	9	Very Hot
500	250	10	Extremely Hot

Any broiling recipes can be used with the grill of the oven, but beware of high-temperature grills.

equivalents for ingredients

all-purpose flour—plain flour
baking sheet—oven tray
buttermilk—ordinary milk
cheesecloth—muslin
coarse salt—kitchen salt
cornstarch—cornflour
eggplant—aubergine

granulated sugar—castor sugar
half and half—12% fat milk
heavy cream—double cream
light cream—single cream
lima beans—broad beans
parchment paper—greaseproof paper
plastic wrap—cling film

scallion—spring onion
shortening—white fat
unbleached flour—strong, white flour
vanilla bean—vanilla pod
zest—rind
zucchini—courgettes or marrow